Without Bosses

First published 2020 by Interventions Inc

Interventions is a not-for-profit, independent left wing book publisher.
For further information:
    www.interventions.org.au
    info@interventions.org.au
    Trades Hall Suite 68
    54 Victoria Street
    Carlton VIC 3053

Design and layout by Viktoria Ivanova
Cover photo from Tribune October 16-22, 1973, photographer unknown. Used with kind permission of The Search Foundation.

For those photographers whose images we used without permission, we tried to find you and couldn't and thank you for your wonderful contributions.

Author: Sam Oldham

Title: Without bosses. Radical Australian Trade Unionism in the 1970s
ISBN: 978-0-6487603-0-6: Paperback

© Sam Oldham 2020

The moral rights of the author have been asserted.
All rights reserved. Except as permitted under the Australian Copyright Act 1968 (for example, a fair dealing for the purposes of study, research, criticism or review), no part of this book may be reproduced, stored in a retrieval system, communicated or transmitted in any form or by any means without prior written permission.

All inquiries should be made to the author.

A catalogue record for this book is available from the National Library of Australia

Without Bosses

Radical Australian Trade Unionism in the 1970s

Sam Oldham

INTERVENTIONS
MELBOURNE

Interventions is produced on the land of the Wurundjeri people of the Kulin Nation. We acknowledge the Traditional Owners of country throughout Australia and recognise their continuing connection to land, waters and culture. We pay our respects to their Elders past, present and emerging. Their land was stolen, never ceded. It always was and always will be Aboriginal land.

'It gives you a bit of an idea of how it would be to work under socialism, without bosses.'

– NSW coal miner & unionist, 1972

The book is dedicated to my grandfather, Hilary Scott, a retired carpenter who would have read it with interest. He passed away as it was being prepared for publication.

CONTENTS

	Acknowledgements	1
	Foreword	3
	Introduction	5
1	Workers in a Climate of Unrest	15
2	Smashing into the 1970s	25
3	Politics and Ideas	39
4	Radical Unionists at the Workplace	57
5	Work Without Bosses	83
6	Worker and Union Ownership	99
7	Radical Unions Beyond the Workplace	113
8	Crisis, Repression and Decline	141
9	Radical Legacies	157
	Endnotes	161
	Bibliography	173

ACKNOWLEDGEMENTS

This book would not have been possible without the support of numerous people. I would like to thank Janey Stone very warmly for accepting the manuscript on behalf of Interventions, for coordinating the project and for leading me through the publication process with patience. My sincere gratitude goes to Michael Lazarus for rescuing the book from limbo and delivering it to Interventions. I am grateful for his feedback on the draft and for his encouragement along the way. My thanks go to Liz Ross for her painstaking efforts in reviewing the final manuscript and for her invaluable feedback. I would like to thank everyone involved with Interventions for publishing the work and keeping the tradition of radical independent publishing alive.

Without Bosses began life some years ago as a Master of Arts thesis at Monash University. It would not have been possible without the help of my dutiful and patient thesis supervisors, Steve Wright and Erik Eklund. I also owe a debt of gratitude to librarians and archivists at Monash University, the University of Wollongong, the State Library of Victoria, the State Library of New South Wales, the National Library, and Katie Wood at the University of Melbourne Archives. I would like to thank all the trade unionists, active and retired, who agreed to talk to me for the project. There are too many to count, but a short list includes Frank Cherry (with the support of the AMWU), Ken Purdham (with the support of the ETU), Malcolm MacDonald, Andrew Dettmer, John Cleary, Jerome Small, George Koletsis, Graeme Watson, Ron Carli, Nando Lelli, Mick Tubbs, Jack Mundey, Pat Johnstone, John Brunskill, Danny Gardiner and Tony Robins.

WITHOUT BOSSES

FOREWORD

Workers' control is a term that can mean many things. From democratic self-management, to worker-ownership, to worker occupations and even strike action—all of these types of actions and formations capture a similar urge. Throughout history, working people have sought to exercise control over their working lives and the economic decisions that affect them. In the present, it seems like this urge has been lost to other concerns. Neo-fascism, the climate crisis, inequality and large-scale unemployment all tear at the fabric of social life. In much of the world, where even the principles of *political* democracy seem in need of protection, the idea of economic democracy seems distant. The idea that our workplaces should be under anything but the autocratic control of bosses and managers remains difficult to shake.

This book gives an account of one period during which the authority of employers and managers *was* shaken. It shows that the decade from the late 1960s in Australia was far and above the most significant period of trade union power and activism in that country, during which workers made serious incursions into the powerful decision-making systems that normally governed their lives. As a result of democratic trade union power, that seemingly inalienable right of bosses, managers, and governments to control the lives of working people was openly challenged. As this book shows, workers in a range of industries challenged the prerogatives of their employers, rejected the official industrial relations apparatus, and defied attempts by the state to police and restrict their activities. Workers experimented with self-management of their workplaces, forms of union and worker-ownership, and new types of strike action over a broad range of concerns. Rather than separate from various social, political and environmental struggles, the workers' movement saw itself as crucial to them.

This was an international phenomenon during the early 1970s. The Institute of Workers' Control in Great Britain was established to trace the radical developments in labour unions occurring there from the late 1960s. Radical labour struggles occurred in many countries throughout Europe and the Americas, shaking the foundations of the employing classes and state power.

In more recent times, the largest strikes in world history have occurred in Third World manufacturing centres upon which Western consumers now depend. In developed countries, ideas of workers' control endure in pockets of economic life. In American cities and towns affected by offshoring and 'deindustrialisation', worker-owned cooperatives have proliferated, intersecting with trade unions in powerful and innovative ways. As Oldham shows, the legacy of the 1970s endures in Australia, with the country's construction union declaring an environmental 'green ban' on the proposed redevelopment of Sydney's Bondi Pavilion as recently as 2017.

The book demonstrates that labour militancy and the practice of worker control is not an antediluvian form drawn from the early 20th century, but a compelling force in more recent times with a powerful legacy in the present. Building a workers' movement requires organisation and careful strategic thinking. Though hard work lies ahead, activists in the present should take heart in the fact that the urge for workers' power is never far from the surface.

Immanuel Ness
Professor of Political Science, Brooklyn College,
City University of New York

INTRODUCTION

The Australian trade union movement boasts a number of world firsts. The use of the word 'green' in political discourse comes from Australian unions. After members of the Builders Labourers Federation (BLF) imposed green bans on environmentally destructive construction projects from 1970, green parties began to spring up around the world, and 'green' became a political orientation. In 1973, BLF members imposed the world's first pink ban on work at Macquarie University, after a student there was expelled for participating in queer activism. In 1972, coal miners in the small New South Wales (NSW) town of South Clifton became the first miners in the world to effectively dismiss their supervisors and take their mine into workers' self-management, giving them, in the words of a participant, 'a bit of an idea of how it would be to work under socialism, without bosses.' That experiment was short lived, but coal miners in Nymboida took similar action three years later. This time, they transferred the mine into full worker-ownership. For the first time in history, a coal mine was managed and owned by its workers through a democratic trade union cooperative.

Similar experiments were tried across a range of industries, from steel work to textiles. Other actions taken by Australian unions reverberated around the world. On the waterfront and on ships, many unionists refused to do any work that supported the war in Vietnam, dictatorships in Greece and Spain, the proliferation of nuclear weapons or the exploitation of workers from developing nations. Through their actions, the power of Australian trade unions was felt internationally.

This book is a history of these and other radical currents in the Australian union movement during the 1970s. What occurred during this decade was a surge in democratic trade union power and, within the surge, a tendency among some trade unionists to challenge the traditional authority of bosses, managers, and even governments, in ways that went well beyond what would typically be expected of trade unions. Many rank-and-file unionists involved in these struggles believed that their workplaces could be managed democratically on a more permanent basis and that ordinary working people should have the right to make social and economic decisions usually made by governments, large company executives, investors and union leaders. Their tactics for achieving this were a mix of old and new. They included occupations and sit-ins of workplaces, work bans with social rather than industrial targets, wildcat strikes, blockades, and even riots and sabotage. In some of the most radical cases, workers 'dismissed' their managers and took over entire factories and workplaces, to demonstrate that they did not need managers and bosses making decisions for them.

The primary task of trade unions in a capitalist economy is to defend workers' interests by negotiating with employers over pay and conditions. For the most part, as Tom Bramble writes,

> Unions are institutions firmly located on the terrain of capitalism, devoted to improving the terms on which labour power is sold within the existing class system rather than striving to transform it.[1]

The structure of modern trade unions contributes to this. Union officials, often former activists from the rank-and-file, tend to develop a different consciousness in their relationship to society and work. Being no longer on the shop floor, it is easy for them to become detached from the daily experiences and struggles of workers. This has been true in Australia as much as elsewhere. Quoting Tom Bramble again:

> As collective bargaining and arbitration became central to industrial relations in the quarter century before World

War One, unions appointed full-time representatives to negotiate for them. These officials developed valuable expertise but, as a result of their removal from the general work force, they have come to play a separate and distinctive role within the labour movement: part of the union but not part of the working class. Their work experiences are different and their wages and conditions are generally better. Over time this layer of negotiating officials has developed into a labour movement bureaucracy which in modern Australia consists of the unions' senior officers (secretaries, assistant secretaries and presidents), field staff (organisers), and professional advisers (lawyers, economists, health and safety specialists etc.).[2]

We can see the conflicting role of the trade union bureaucracy in the various union struggles that occurred during the radical upsurge. Sometimes, officials did provide leadership and support to the rank and file, particularly when they came under pressure from union members who organised in shop committees and other structures. Sometimes, however, they held back support, shored up control and even sabotaged workers' initiatives. At the higher levels of trade union bureaucracy, such as in the Trades Hall Councils and the Australian Council of Trade Unions (ACTU), this became more likely, often resulting in bitter disputes between rank-and-file union members and the peak union bodies. In this situation, struggles from below, from the shop floor, are of tremendous importance. And they were not wanting.

Trade unions are also not homogeneous organisations. This book shows that, if unions are allowed to be genuinely democratic organisations controlled by their members rather than by entrenched officials and oppressive legal regimes, they can be put to use in radical ways in the service of ordinary people.

The radical potential of trade unions is a strong thread in history. Historically, revolutionary trade unions have been organisations by which working people have sought to seize control of their workplaces

UK Workers control poster 1960s.

and industries to build a socialist society from the bottom up. We might think of the revolutionary Industrial Workers of the World (the Wobblies) in Australia and elsewhere during the 1910s, or the anarchist trade unions that organised large parts of Spain during the revolution of the late 1930s. While these histories are quite different to the struggles of the 1970s, they show that trade unions can and do take different forms, including radical ones. Rather than indulging in nostalgia, we should take hope from the fact that the corporatised unions of today maintain the same basic principles that all trade unions do: they are organisations composed of workers, funded by workers and (at least in principle, if not always in practice) controlled by workers.

Many factors underlie the mass militancy and self-activity of the Australian working class in the 1970s. By 1969, the power of the union movement had been growing for three decades. Around half of all workers were in unions, and full employment had given them confidence to take action with a low fear of being unemployed. Spurred by a wave of popular social activism from the late 1960s, 1970s workers were infused by a new mood of rebellion and defiance. Trade unionists wanted the right to be involved in the decisions affecting their working lives and the communities in which they lived. They experimented with new ways to organise workplaces, thus partially challenging alienation from capitalist decision-making systems. They challenged the assumption that corporate executives, business owners, wealthy investors and governments had the exclusive right to control industry and govern society. Workplace committees and community alliances became new spaces for democratic power and popular decision making. Many trade unionists adopted radical ideas about capitalism and work, and radical trade unionism appeared again on the Australian industrial and political landscape.

Radical currents within Australian trade unionism were often referred to collectively as a movement for workers' control, a term that was adopted from the UK and used by left wing trade unionists, members of the Communist Party of Australia (CPA) and even parts of the media and public. Conferences were dedicated to discussing and understanding it. British trade unionists and academics had, in 1968, established an Institute for Workers' Control, to analyse and record, in the words of its founders, 'the growth of an explicit trade-union demand for workers' control over the major decisions involved in modern industry.'[3] The idea inspired followers in Australia, where it was discussed and debated among local proponents. Denis Freney, a left wing member of the Communist Party, observed in 1973 that:

> The right to strike and to form unions are forms of workers' control, limiting the bosses' power …What is new today is that workers feel the need to go beyond these traditional, partly accepted instances of workers' control to tackle new, formerly unquestioned 'rights' of the boss … the attempt to impose control over different aspects of the power of the bosses and the ruling class (e.g., the bosses' right to sack) … or what piece of environment to destroy, or what war to fight.[4]

Jack Hutson, a research officer for the Amalgamated Engineering Union (AEU), defined workers' control in 1969 along similar lines:

> the extension of the right of the trade unions particularly in the workshop, through their representatives, to have an effective say in decisions made in respect to such matters as trade unionism, safety, welfare, discipline, wage fixation, appointment of supervisory staff, deployment of labour, technological changes, hiring and firing and access to financial records.

These changes Hutson viewed as a 'tall order when put against the usually recognised trade union rights.'[5] Proponents of workers' control usually associated it with workers' self-management at the enterprise level and sometimes with forms of worker-ownership, such as union cooperatives. Joe Owens, a leading figure in the radical NSW Builders Labourers Federation (NSWBLF), described workers' control as 'part of the wider political movement for self-management', and others shared this view.[6] Carter L. Goodrich, in his fascinating study of the British shop

BLF green bans demonstration 1970s.
Unknown photographer.

stewards' movement, *The Frontier of Control* (1921), also used the term *workers' control*, which he described as 'a bewildering variety of rights and claims' unified by a direct challenge to the rights of employers to control industry.[7] The same could be said for the radical trade unionism of the 1970s. The rank and file and sections of the union bureaucracy challenged the rights of employers to control industry, in new and radical ways and to an extent not seen for decades.

Workers' control as a concept was a cause for much concern among business, political and media circles. A Liberal Party pamphlet published in September 1973 warned that 'workers' control has ceased to be an empty phrase or an implied threat' and that 'the muzzling and control of management by worker committees' had 'challenged the ability of employers to make men redundant' and asserted 'the right of workers to elect their own foremen, decide what kind of goods a factory should produce and have access to the employers' books to decide what the level of profit should be.' A *Sydney Morning Herald* reporter, writing about the new radicalism of the labour movement in July 1973, noted that it had 'a common theme of encroachment upon managerial authority' and that 'workers' control is already affecting us all'.[8] Quickly, radical trade unionism struck fear into the hearts of large employers, the rich and powerful, and their lackeys in politics and the press.

This book crafts a narrative that allows for discussion of the various actions and attitudes that reflected the radical union tendencies of the 1970s. It begins with the destruction of the industrial 'penal powers' in 1969 because of mass strike action – an event that rendered governments powerless to suppress industrial action as they had for two decades, through heavy fines and arrests of union leaders. Most radical union action occurred in the four to five years following the penal powers strike, in what Tom Bramble refers to as the great 'flood tide' of Australian trade union activism. Within this flood tide emerged the various green (and other) bans, occupations, work-ins and takeovers, union and worker cooperative experiments that characterised a more radical trade unions', or workers', control.

By the late 1970s, radical expressions of trade unionism had become less common. A bookend to the narrative was seen in June 1979, when an attempt by Western Australian police to charge metal unionists with holding an illegal meeting was quickly reversed by the prospect of mass strike action, in a direct repetition of the penal powers affair. A two-year strike wave followed. Although it was more concerned with the bread-and-butter issues we might normally associate with trade unionism, major workplace occupations and blockades did occur. Even at the end of the decade, the Fraser government refused to use the punitive anti-union laws it had introduced, for fear that unions would just shake them off. It was not until the 1980s that employers and governments moved to destroy the union movement, with considerable success.

In the decades since the 1970s, the power of the union movement has been greatly eroded, and many of the gains made during that period have been rolled back. Now, union coverage is at historic lows, with less than 15 percent of the workforce belonging to unions, and most of those in the public sector. The capacity of rank-and-file union members to take direct action is often buried beneath layers of organisational bureaucracy, which is itself entrenched by increasingly vicious anti-union regulatory regimes. It has been said that, for the first time since they were forged out of the fiery industrial struggles of the nineteenth century, trade unions in

Australia face the real prospect of ceasing to exist as meaningful economic and political actors.[9] Bitter repression of unions by governments and their corporate supporters continues. Legislation recently introduced by the Coalition government – called, in truly Orwellian terms, the Ensuring Integrity Bill – would allow unions to be deregistered for submitting late paperwork. As unions have been pushed further and further to the margins of social and economic life, popular apathy and ignorance about unions have contributed to their decline.

It is easy to understand why many trade unionists look back on the 1970s with nostalgia, but we should be wary. The 1970s was far from a perfect time. Women were excluded from large parts of the workforce and the union movement in ways that they are not today; many of the industries that are the focus of this book were almost exclusively male. Men were paid more, and gendered notions of work kept women confined to lower paying jobs and certain social roles. Many men in unions, progressive though they were in other ways, did not do enough to support their female comrades. It would be untrue to say that the decades since have represented absolute progress, but the 1970s was undoubtedly a more difficult period for many workers belonging to various marginalised social groups, including Aboriginal and Torres Strait Islander people, queer and gender diverse people, people with disabilities and non-European (non-white) immigrants. Even immigrants from southern and eastern Europe were not immune from racism and alienation. The average workplace was hotter, louder, dirtier and more dangerous in that period than it is today; this progress is due largely to the struggles waged by unionists in the decades since.

Above all, the 1970s tell a story of ordinary people who, by organising at their workplaces and coordinating action across industries and trades, challenged systems of exploitation and oppression through direct action. The actions of trade unionists in that period stand as a testament to the possibility of democratic alternatives to the corporate domination and bureaucratic inertia of contemporary political and economic life. Looking around the world today, we see that workers and other oppressed groups can and do rise up and challenge their rulers in the most unexpected and unpredictable ways. They invent new forms of radicalism or reinterpret old forms for the new conditions they face. The radicalism described in this book is unlikely to appear again in exactly the form as in the 1970s. But we can be sure that there will be new periods of mass activism, radicalism and struggle from rank-and-file workers and their allies. Workers will again realise that they can take over and run their workplaces themselves, without bosses. Meanwhile, I hope that those struggling and fighting in Australia today find inspiration and renewed courage from this account of the radical trade unionism of the 1970s.

CHAPTER 1
Workers in a Climate of Unrest

Australian events from the late 1960s were part of a wave of popular activism that swept much of the world. Parliaments, dictatorships, the military-industrial complex, bosses, the patriarchy, racism and white supremacy, colonialism, homophobia and tedious work – all were called into contest by popular social movements and bitterly, even violently, opposed. Opposition to the catastrophic American-led war in Vietnam was an important part of the new popular mood. For the first time in history, the television brought graphic scenes of the violence unleashed on the people of Vietnam to viewers around the world in real time. In the US, something of an epicentre for global unrest, the prospect of military conscription led to seething discontent among many young people, expressed through mass demonstrations, riots, and underground actions by Weather Underground and other groups. Many of the mass social movements of the era either had their origins directly in anti-war activism or were inspired by it.

American political and business leaders, presiding over the most powerful state in world history, felt besieged. The Trilateral Commission, an elite think tank assembled by David Rockefeller and intellectuals from the US, Japan and Western Europe, released a report in 1975 revealing the sense of alarm with which Western governments viewed developments in their societies. Called *The Crisis of Democracy*, the report railed against 'changes in social values' which included 'greater scepticism towards political leaders and institutions with greater alienation from the political

Strikers demand the release of Clarrie O'Shea 1969.
Photo courtesy University of Melbourne Archives.

processes.' It seethed at 'the derogation of leadership, the challenging of authority, and the unmasking and delegitimation of established institutions' by the public. The 'governability of societies' by established political and business elites was becoming untenable; no longer was a quiet and detached citizenship content to vote every few years and leave decision making to politicians and state planners. With the new enthusiasm for protest, democracy had got out of hand.[10]

Worker and union struggles were a part of this new activism. In France, the 1968 student protests inspired strikes and worker occupations that led to the largest general strike in world history. In Italy, the Hot Autumn of 1969 was characterised by mass wildcat strikes and occupations in the factories of the country's north. In the UK, industrial struggle rose to its highest point in half a century. Waves of official and unofficial strikes over wages and conditions were coordinated by rank-and-file bodies across a range of industries. Such was the strength of the surge that, when Prime Minister Edward Heath called the 1974 election, he ran on a platform of 'Who Governs Britain?' – the unions or the government – and lost.

British unions embraced radical new tactics and rejuvenated old ones.

Between June and October 1971, the proposed closure of the Upper Clydeside shipyards in Glasgow led to the world's first work-in, when workers took over the shipyard and continued work in defiance of its closure. This tactic led to a spate of similar actions. In 1968, thinkers associated with the left of the British Labour Party, the Communist Party of Great Britain and the unions established the Institute for Workers' Control to analyse the growth of radical unionism in that country. Left wing political forces gained influence among British workers during this period. The Communist Party was still a major activist force in engineering and other militant industrial sectors. Most workers, however, although enthusiastic for industrial militancy, remained unaffiliated. Chris Harman notes: 'the largest minority among trade union activists was not formally organised at all' but 'was made up of the many thousands of workers who had basic socialist class commitment, without any fixed political affiliation.'[11]

Strikes over social issues became more common internationally. In famous cases, such as the 1968 strike by women at the Dagenham Ford plant in the UK, or the major strike by African American sanitation workers in Memphis the same year, workers brought struggles for social emancipation to their workplaces. Many strikes were simply against the oppressive nature of the boss or the boring and tedious nature of work. The authors of a pamphlet about a wildcat strike at a Dodge manufacturing plant in June 1974 capture the mood well:

> We were excited by the collective decision of thousands of Chrysler employees to deny the authority of daily wage labor and, for even four days, to say no to the demands of the alarm clock, the production line, bosses, union bureaucrats, judges and cops. In a society where daily activity serves so much the interests of others and so little our own, the efforts of so many to reclaim even short-run control over their lives seemed worth writing about.[12]

In New Zealand, the introduction of a general nil wage order (no wage increase) by the arbitration authority in 1968 provoked a minor general strike in Wellington and a small riot outside the parliament building. In

18 WITHOUT BOSSES

Trade unionists demonstrate for release of Clarrie O'Shea 1969.
Unknown photographer.

subsequent years, union faith in the arbitration court was destroyed, and there was a surge in industrial action and direct bargaining.

Australia entered a similar period of unrest from the late 1960s. The Vietnam War and conscription had much to do with this, politicising and radicalising broader sections of society. A visiting American scholar observed 'the spilling over of Vietnam and conscription from the strict area of external affairs into other concerns of public policy and behaviour' in 'an awakening which has permeated both the mass public and the attentive-interested sectors of the public.' These 'destabilizing contributions of the Vietnam-conscription controversy' had 'injected a new, or at least newly advertised, ideological dimension into a well-aggregated society.'[13] This was true of earlier periods of social and industrial unrest: a period of labour radicalism led by the Wobblies coincided with WWI in Australia, while a major strike wave followed World War II (WWII).

The Vietnam War had a direct impact on the Australian labour movement. Many workers joined the anti-war movement, and anti-war activism became a feature of workplace struggle. Waterfront and shipping unions imposed a number of bans in opposition to the war, while the Stop Work to Stop the War campaign ran throughout 1969 and 1970, implemented by workers across a range of industries. The idea of being drafted into the army and shipped off to be killed led many young men to turn to radical ideas, including dissent and disdain for authority. For those who were in unions, this easily translated into disdain for the authority of the boss, especially in industries involved in assisting the war. At the Cerberus Naval Dockyards on the outskirts of Melbourne, maintenance workers banned all work on the officers' toilets in response to naval police targeting them with speed cameras. Tony Robins, a shop steward for the Electrical Trades Union (ETU) at the yards, recalls:

> we weren't going to be bullied by people who think they're in authority. So we black banned the Police headquarters and their toilets blocked up, and we wouldn't fix them. And they had sewage running out … They'd bring in a contractor; we'd stop the contractor at the gate.

Global social movements had started to have an impact on Australian society in the late 1960s and 1970s, and these also circulated with labour struggles. Women's liberation challenged institutionalised gender discrimination from employers and union officials. A movement for Aboriginal land rights and cultural revival developed, supported by strikes of Aboriginal workers and solidarity actions by predominantly white workers. In January 1970, the first openly homosexual political group was launched; the Australasian Lesbian Movement was an Australian chapter of the American lesbian group, Daughters of Bilitis.

Ideas of self-organisation and direct action cross-pollinated the trade union movement from new social movements. Judy Gillet, a teachers' unionist, wrote in *Australian Left Review* in August 1973:

> very many similarities exist between the struggle for
> workers' control and other forms of social struggle,
> e.g., women's liberation and environmental struggles,
> etc., which are also struggles for self-determination,
> anti-authoritarianism, anti-exploitation and
> anti-divisiveness.[14]

Likewise, John Cleary, a builders' labourer and CPA member, recalls that social struggle:

> has relation to workers' control. I think what occurred
> in '68 in France caused an awakening on so many levels.
> Then of course feminism became a large discussion point
> on the left. The rights of gays, bisexuals, everything that
> we previously held was questioned, in terms of social
> behaviour, including the notion of the master-servant.

The workers' control tendency was directly rooted in this new social ferment. As some sectors of society began to think more critically of systems of domination and control, many workers began to turn the same critical eye to the institution of private enterprise.

It became more common for individual union members to challenge union leaders. In late 1969, Zelda D'Aprano, a long-time member of the CPA and employee of the Australasian Meat Industry Employees Union (AMIEU), took direct action after an Arbitration Court decision on equal pay which would only benefit 5 percent of women workers. She chained herself to the Commonwealth Building in central Melbourne, demanding equal pay for women. When she challenged the AMIEU's acceptance of the decision which left most women on only 75 percent of the male wage, the AMIEU leadership unceremoniously dismissed her from her job in the union office. When she complained to the leadership of the CPA, the party upheld the AMIEU's decision, provoking her resignation.

A year later, D'Aprano and other activists drew attention to unequal pay when they refused to pay more than 75 percent of the fare on the Melbourne tramways. In 1972, women broke into the Australian Iron & Steel plant at Port Kembla and worked for several hours in a campaign for equal access to employment. In 1973, all women were laid off at the Draffin-Everhot stove manufacturing plant in Melbourne, including the shop steward. In response, the sacked women blockaded the gates of the plant. Before long, they were supported by many women from women's liberation and 200 workers from a nearby metal plant. Disillusioned with male dominance of the trade unions, D'Aprano formed the Women's Action Committee in 1970, to push women's issues within unions and employment.

The late 1960s and the 1970s was also a period of intergenerational conflict and youth revolt, as young people experimented with new drugs, new relationships and radical political ideas. They drove student protest, fuelled the anti-war movement and had a profound impact on industrial relations. *Tribune* observed in 1972 that 'the youth revolt has affected large numbers of working youth' and 'has in the main relied on spontaneity.' A shop steward with the ETU, recalling a surge in young apprentices joining his union, could attribute this only to 'the mood of the times.' In December 1971, 80 apprentices at GM-Holden Elizabeth South Australia (SA) occupied their administration building to force company recognition of their shop stewards. Similar campaigns occurred at the GM-Holden Woodville plant, the Whyalla shipyard and the Osborne power station. The American labour sociologist Harry Braverman attributed a new 'active dissatisfaction' with work in the 1970s to 'the characteristics of the workers—younger, more years of schooling, "infected" by the new generational restlessness.'[15] Anti-war sentiment propelled some radical unionists into representative positions. Nando Lelli, a well-known socialist and rank-and-file activist, was elected as the Federated Ironworkers Association (FIA) shop steward at the massive Australian Iron and Steel (AI&S) plant in Port Kembla in 1970, to the dismay of the company. Lelli's militant Rank and File ticket won the Port Kembla branch election, largely because of growing anti-war sentiment; ticket members had consistently led opposition to the war throughout the later 1960s.

Social and political upheaval, both foreign and domestic, was seminal in the labour radicalism that emerged in Australia in the period after 1969. Many Australian workers were inspired by, and involved in, the radical activities of anti-war activists, students and young people, as well as the struggles of women, Aboriginal Australians, LGBT people, and other marginalised groups. Similarly, international events were a source of inspiration and encouragement. While Australian workers responded primarily to local conditions, their actions did not occur in isolation from the global upsurge. Australian workers set new standards for what workers could achieve.

CHAPTER 2
Smashing into the 1970s

THE POST-WAR BOOM

After a bitter wave of strikes between 1945 and 1949, Australian workers entered a state of relative complacency. Perceived as the triumph of Keynesianism across developed nations, the period from the early 1950s through to the late 1960s was one in which global capitalism enjoyed unprecedented success. In Australia, the post-war economic boom brought rising wages and full employment, and access to affordable land and housing made the prospect of home ownership realistic for many workers for the first time. Mass manufacturing, the backbone of the economic recovery, made an abundance of consumer goods available at relatively low cost, while low interest rates allowed easy access to consumer credit. Rapid growth in vehicle manufacturing meant that large numbers of Australians could own cars for the first time. Craig McGregor, a popular journalist and cultural observer, wrote that Australians were 'content with the present, eager to forget the past, optimistic about the future … The climate of class warfare is rapidly receding.'[16]

At the same time, from the end of the 1940s, the government ramped up repression of trade unions. In 1947, the Chifley Labor government granted penal powers to the Arbitration Court, allowing it to fine unions for taking strike action. Two years later, Chifley used the military to smash the 1949 coal strike, before losing a federal election in December. The new Menzies Liberal government escalated repression of trade unions further.

Menzies amended the *Conciliation and Arbitration Act* to allow for bans clauses, or no strike clauses, in industrial awards. Tom Bramble explains:

> The bans clauses offered advantages to the Menzies Government that jailing union leaders did not. The latter action created an important propaganda opportunity for the unions ... The bans clauses, by contrast, were put into effect by the Arbitration Commission and enforced by the Industrial Court, which were nominally at arm's length from the government. Further, the measure involved bleeding the unions financially, which lacked the dramatic effect of marching union leaders into jail.[17]

The penal powers served as the cornerstone of the post-war industrial relations apparatus. They curbed the activities of rank-and-file militants, and officials turned to pursuing gains through arbitration. Even left wing union officials sought to curtail the activities of their members in order to avoid penalties. AEU officials were often forced to restrain their rank-and-file members. John Halfpenny, a CPA member and Victorian State Secretary of the Amalgamated Metal Workers' Union (AMWU) throughout the 1970s, lamented that the penal powers had 'robbed workers of the right to struggle and turned Union Officials into strike breakers.'[18] As a result, the period from 1956 to 1968 was one of protracted labour movement restraint.

Australia became an industrial economy in the post-WWII decades. Mass manufacturing expanded significantly, led by the vehicle industry and supporting industries such as iron and steel. Factory employment grew by one-third between 1953–54 and 1966–67, to 1.3 million. By the early 1970s, manufacturing and heavy industries employed over half a million people as fitters and turners, engineers, mechanics or process workers in the massive car plants and steelworks. Heavy manufacturing, such as shipbuilding and automotive manufacturing, was concentrated in Victoria and NSW, particularly in the Melbourne and Sydney metropolitan areas. As a result, unions in these industries were particularly powerful. The AEU, with 86,000 members, stood in 1969 as the second

Vehicle builders at AMI Port Melbourne factory on strike 1973.
Photo courtesy Socialist Alternative.

largest union in the country, after the Australian Workers' Union (AWU). The union grew stronger through amalgamations with sheet metal workers in 1973 and shipwrights in 1976.

The construction industry saw an unprecedented boom from the late 1960s through to at least 1974. Much of the development was concentrated in the Sydney and Melbourne metropolitan areas. Full employment and rising wages encouraged militancy. In high-development areas like Sydney, developers demanded quick completion of speculative projects, their reluctance to stall development giving leverage to the NSWBLF and other building industry unions. In the first five months of 1971, for example, three out of four working days lost across industry were recorded in NSW, and 45 percent of the total days lost in all industries were from the building industry. Economic conditions, combined with the success of militant industrial action, attracted large numbers of builders' labourers into the union. Between 1969 and 1971, membership of the NSWBLF rose nationally by 136 percent, compared with an overall union increase of 7 percent over the same period. The concentration of development projects in central Sydney meant that NSWBLF members on different jobs were in close proximity. Large urban jobs were often the most militant, and workers could share stories at local pubs and hotels, as well as assisting each other's actions across different sites.

With the development of very large-scale urban projects, small and medium construction companies were increasingly displaced by massive, often multinational, companies, and the sheer size of new development projects distanced construction workers from managers and owners. There was also a proliferation of subcontracting; this had always been financially riskier, but that status was exacerbated because boom conditions attracted underprepared subcontracting outfits into the industry. New development also heightened the importance of demolition and excavation work, so the unions were important in the early stages of projects and were well positioned to impose environmental and social bans.

WORKERS TAKE ADVANTAGE

Conditions of full employment gave significant power to workers in unions. Many companies would rather give in to union demands for better pay and conditions than stop production for a strike. The industrial relations manager at GM-Holden Elizabeth recalled: 'We had the attitude then that we would do all in our power to keep production going', which gave shop stewards 'an environment to take up a whole range of issues.' At the same time, many workers could afford to lose a few days of pay for a strike, and the threat of being sacked for industrial action carried less weight when other work could be found relatively easily. To win gains more quickly, rank-and-file trade unionists moved away from the system of industrial awards, turning instead to over-award agreements negotiated directly with employers. This turn to direct bargaining spurred growth in rank-and-file organisation and provided fertile conditions for the expansion of union activity into areas of managerial prerogative. Nonetheless, higher wages were the determinant factor in the surge in rank-and-file self-activity; in the words of Frank Cherry, a prominent AEU organiser:

> Without local struggle for wage growth, the shopfloor movement would grow very weak. In many cases people would lose their desire to fight for their rights on the job. ... I think that the whole democratic base of the union would be at stake.

The movement for workers' control was indivisible from this surge in shopfloor organisation and the democratisation of unions as a result of the wages struggle.[19]

The growing power and confidence of ordinary trade unionists provoked alarm in employers and conservative commentators. The right wing *Courier Mail* in Brisbane, reporting on a strike at Evans Deakin shipyards in August 1969, warned that:

> The real trouble is rank and file control ... The campaign is being run by a bunch of stirrers ... Every time the Metal Trades Federation makes a decision, the rank and file knock it over.

The conservative arbitration commissioner A. E. Woodward argued the following year that 'one of the biggest dangers in union affairs today is the spread of so-called "participatory democracy" which means, in effect, rule by mass meetings.' Mass meetings as a tool for participatory decision making came to the fore in the mid-1960s. Laurie Carmichael, Victorian State Secretary of the AEU throughout the 1960s, described mass meetings in 1964 as 'a new development in the union.' Union officials were increasingly relegated to positions of either sympathy with, or opposition to, rank-and-file power growing within their own organisations.[20]

Migrant workers played a key role in these developments. Australia saw large-scale immigration in the post-war decades, with migrants representing as much as 80 percent of the increase in the workforce from the late 1940s to the early 1960s, particularly in manufacturing. Migrant workers contributed much to Australian union radicalism. The caricature of the 'pommie' shop steward became pervasive, as militant British unionists migrated to Australia and entered the local movement. Large numbers migrated from Turkey and Greece after revolutions and military coups disrupted their home countries. Ron Carli, a member of the Vehicle Builders' Employees' Federation (VBEF), believes that migrants from Greece and Turkey had a 'different understanding of unionism' and a 'totally different idea of how to run a strike' in that 'you make your point.'

Migrants from non-English speaking backgrounds also experienced frustrations. Many took work on tedious factory lines and had a limited ability to communicate with their co-workers and supervisors. Such migrants, for example, comprised more than 80 percent of participants in the Ford Broadmeadows (Melbourne) riot of 1973. In many cases, the newness of these workers to the country, the difficulty of the work they were expected to do and their social alienation and exclusion meant that they felt less commitment than Australian-born workers to the formal structures of trade unions. They often brought radical attitudes. The construction industry boom attracted large numbers of migrants. Historically, the industry had been a stepping stone for them, allowing them to move into other jobs. Higher wages in the industry meant that many stayed, no doubt contributing to the radical culture of the union.

Often, it fell to shopfloor unionists to organise migrants. A strike committee at Ford Broadmeadows in 1969 facilitated cooperation between Greek, Italian, Lebanese, Yugoslav and Turkish workers, who made 'decisions at well-run meetings' and 'in providing interpreters for the many migrant workers.' Similarly, at B&D Doors in Melbourne, workers organised 'a shop committee along ethnic lines', in which 'ethnic groups each elected a representative to the shop committee' who would 'explain proposals and decisions of mass meetings to migrants in their own language.' The journals of all major militant unions during the period published important information in a number of languages.[21]

SHOP COMMITTEES AND RANK-AND-FILE MILITANCY

Shop committees were at the core of union militancy from the late 1960s. Sometimes called shop steward committees, combined union committees or site committees (in construction), these were organisations made up of workers from one or several unions, elected by workers in individual workplaces. Area committees, most common in large government industries, were organisations of union members across multiple factories and workplaces. Shop committees had first appeared in Australia during the union radicalism of the early 1900s. The Wobblies had agitated for shop committees in Australia, while other workers were inspired by the rise of the British shop stewards' movement during the same period. In the decades following WWII, shop committees proliferated throughout much of government-owned heavy industry, including munitions, railways, aircraft and shipbuilding. From the 1960s, they spread wildly from the nationalised industries throughout the private sector. By the 1970s, most small and medium enterprises in manufacturing and related industries were organised by shop committees.

Officially, shop committees existed to improve communication between union officials and union members, or to maintain workplace conditions affecting members of multiple unions where that did not breach awards and agreements. The ACTU frequently reminded shop committees that they were bound by awards and agreements and were not supposed to engage in direct bargaining; that authority belonged to union officials. In reality, shop committees often engaged in direct bargaining over wages and conditions, leading large-scale campaigns in government manufacturing industries, dockyards and elsewhere by the mid-1960s. For many workers, shop committees represented a form of direct democracy at the workplace, allowing them to circumvent both their boss and, if necessary, the apathy of their own union officials. Where they were not within the jurisdiction of any individual union, they represented alternative centres of allegiance. The ACTU, fearing that shop committees were undermining the authority of union leaderships, attempted to bring them under control with a *Charter for Shop Committees* in 1961 and by banning area committees in 1963. This had little effect. Employers also saw the dangers that shop committees might pose to their authority. The Metal Trades Industry Association bemoaned what it called the 'plant by plant duress' of the shop committee movement. The Victorian Chamber of Manufacturers and the Metal Trades Employers' Federation advised their member companies not to recognise committees in their factories.

For more radical workers, shop committees presented a means by which workers' control could be established at the enterprise level. A shop steward on the powerful Kenworth Trucks shop committee in Melbourne 'saw the committee as a real alternative to the bosses' management' in 1976, while another steward remarked that: 'We could run the place better than they do.' John Cleary, who spent the early 1970s reporting on shop committees in the rank-and-file metal workers' journal, *Link*, recalls that 'almost every place had a committee of some sort or another.' One example was a powerful area committee established at the Wattie Pict food factory in outer Melbourne in June 1975, 'to be more effective in fighting for their log of claims' and to stop management 'playing one shift against another, one factory against another.' Most shop committees developed an annual log of claims, which they would present to management. Usually, without the protection of penal powers, employers settled claims in the workers' favour. Shop committees became effective forms of worker self-activity and democratic organisation, whose proliferation employers could do little to contain.

While shop committees did represent a threat to union leaderships, union officials responded to committees in different ways, largely driven by differences in their political affiliations. The AEU leadership, dominated by the CPA, endorsed shop committees unequivocally as 'the means by which increased workers' control over the employers can be exercised at the point of production.' Officials of the Blacksmiths & Boilermakers' Society and the Sheet Metal Workers' Union took similar approaches. After their merger into the giant AMWU in 1973, organisers of the new union talked openly of their hopes that AMWU shop committees would 'infect' members of other unions with their enthusiasm for activism. The AEU had always maintained a more decentralised structure than related unions, one that was conducive to the development of shop committees. AEU District Committees had a degree of autonomy, acting as quasi-independent organisations. District Committees, in turn, encouraged the autonomy of shop stewards. Ted Gnatenko, a prominent AEU steward at the massive GM-Holden plant in Elizabeth, quipped that, by the late 1960s, stewards were the 'masters of the union, and the organisers were the servants.' Jack Hutson, AEU research officer, was keenly aware of the rank-and-file nature of the shop committee movement, warning in 1965 that attempts by union officials and employers to contain the activities of shop committees 'risks being at loggerheads with them' because they 'fill a deeply felt need of the rank and file dictated by the hard facts of industrial life itself.'[22]

The rank-and-file upsurge provoked tensions within conservative unions. The leadership of the FIA, the third-largest union in the country, was vehemently anti-Communist. Laurie Short, associated with Catholic anti-Communist forces, had defeated the Communist leadership of the FIA in 1951 and retained its presidency until 1982. National Secretary Harry Hurrell had previously been a foreman and security guard at AIS. The FIA leadership hated shop committees, seeing them as Communist cells in disguise. Short regularly warned members against joining them, while Hurrell condemned them as anarchists. In the vehicle industry, VBEF officials attempted to block combined-union committees organised by the AEU, leading to bitter attacks on the union leadership by VBEF militants.

Despite their leaderships, members of the FIA and VBEF were active at the shop floor, inspired by their peers in left wing unions and the surge in rank-and-file activity generally. In many cases, officials of these unions were hamstrung. In Port Kembla, FIA leaders sought constantly to undermine the radical branch at AI&S. They circulated stories suggesting that Nando Lelli was receiving money from the Soviet Union and eventually tried to expel him for joining a combined-union shop committee not recognised by the ACTU. The *Sydney Morning Herald* decried the perceived fact that 'in parts of Australia ... we are approaching a situation intolerably close to industrial anarchy.'[23] Despite their efforts, employers and conservative union officials could no longer rely on arbitration to police the activities of workers in the absence of the industrial penal powers.

Shop committees were supported by a growing number of closed shop agreements, typically enforced by committees themselves. Closed union shops, in which all employees at the workplace must belong to a union, first became prominent in Australia during the radical union struggles of the late 19th century and have existed since that time in industries such as shipping and mining. Earlier struggles over union hire, however, paled in comparison to those in the late 1960s and 1970s. Militant trade unionists considered union control over hiring at the enterprise to be vital to the integrity of trade unionism. A prominent saying during the period, that 'if you haven't got a closed shop, you haven't got a union', was not taken lightly.

Stories of rank-and-file workers enforcing union hire filled the pages of union journals. Often, they provoked bitter conflicts with employers. For example, after Queensland Alumina Limited locked workers out during a dispute over union hire in 1972, *Tribune* accused the company of:

> smashing the site and delegates' committees, which have developed the workers' rights to an on the spot say in what goes on, along with elements of workers' control of site conditions and labour hire.

The employer demanded that: 'if there is to be a resumption of work it must be with union officials in control, and control must be taken out of the hands of the site committees'; they would 'no longer tolerate union control of labour hire', because 'selection of the workforce must be the responsibility of employers alone.' Rank-and-file control was a source of enormous consternation for the company, who claimed that 'militant workers had taken control of the situation and the unions had not been able to effectively control their membership' and requested that 'trade union officials be permanently stationed in Gladstone.'[24]

In the NSW construction industry, the NSWBLF leadership launched a 'no ticket no start' campaign in 1970. Targeting non-unionists and non-financial union members, as well as any new labour, the union held 'show-card days' throughout September and October. Rank-and-file unionists confronted non-union workers on worksites. As a result, by the end of October, the NSW Public Works Department was a closed shop, and other construction sites in the city and North Sydney areas were strictly closed shop areas. The NSWBLF declared that all sites in the state would soon follow suit.

After individual construction companies failed to break union hire arrangements, the Master Builders Association (MBA) locked out 6,000 labourers on 800 projects across Sydney in May 1973. In the press, the MBA declared that it was 'in a state of war' with the NSWBLF over the issues of union hire and permanency – the union's incursions into employer prerogatives represented 'a direct confrontation on the employer's democratic and undeniable right to select his own employees.'[25] With virtually the entire NSW construction industry in a state of deadlock, the Federal government established an independent inquiry which ended the lockouts and saw a resumption of union power in the area of hiring.

In 1971, a campaign by the Transport Workers Union (TWU) to enforce full union membership among SA bus drivers provoked an employer counterassault, bringing the state's public transport system into deadlock. When the union banned all work in bus companies that employed non-union labour, the major companies went to court. The conflict culminated in a major confrontation. On one side, a mass meeting of several thousand transport workers resolved to take strike action, with the support of other unions, and a mass demonstration marched through central Adelaide. In response, SA's largest corporate employers, including GM-Holden, Kelvinator and Simpson Pope, threatened retrenchments. Within days, the bus companies dropped their civil action, while the TWU was forced to settle for having 'preference to unionists' arrangements inserted into their industrial award.

The turn to direct action, yielding success, led to less reliance on arbitration. Justice Beattie, President of the NSW Industrial Commission, noted: 'the significant thing is that, in the majority of cases, direct action has been successful – and this success has bred further direct action.' A prolonged strike at the AI&S Kwinana steelworks in 1970 ended with an Industrial Commission ruling in favour of the company, sparking fears that unions would turn more forcefully against the state arbitration system altogether.

In 1969, the 'penal powers', first imposed by the Federal Labor government in 1947 and used to harass trade unions with fines for two decades, were defeated through mass strike action. When Clarrie O'Shea, Victorian State Secretary of the Tramways union, was arrested in May for refusing to pay fines imposed on his union for strike action, hundreds of thousands of workers went on strike. They called for his release and for the repeal of the penal powers. Pressure had been building before the O'Shea case, with the major left wing metal unions announcing the previous year that they would no longer pay fines. After an anonymous benefactor paid his fines, O'Shea was released, and the penal powers were a dead letter.

The defeat of the penal powers sparked a torrent of shopfloor activity across industry between 1969 and 1974. Metal workers made more gains through direct action in this period than they had through arbitration in the entire period since 1952. In 1974, transport workers won the largest single wage increase in Australian history. Penal powers had protected managerial prerogatives. Jack Hutson noted, weeks prior to the O'Shea case, that use of the penal powers to end strikes in response to sacked unionists had:

> shown what a powerful bulwark is the arbitration system to encroachment on managerial rights, and this is a formidable limiting factor to the achievement of workers' control.

A crisis in employer and state authority ensued. In the midst of the unrest, Joe Palmada, a prominent Communist Party figure, noted that:

> the present movement received tremendous impetus from the penal powers strike ... which has paralysed the system of compulsory arbitration, opening the way for new offensives by the workers.

Malcolm MacDonald, a convenor of the Newport Power Station Shop Committee, later an organiser for the Federal Engine Drivers and Firemen's Association (FEDFA), describes an 'enormous' and immediate surge of workplace activity, with employers powerless to confront it. MacDonald recalls responding to a strike at the BHP South Melbourne plant in 1970 and describes the helplessness of the foreman, who could only helplessly repeat: 'This is madness. This is madness.'[26]

While militancy was strongest in traditional blue-collar industries, an unprecedented surge occurred in white-collar unionism, with teachers' unions at the forefront. Victorian teachers struck for the first time ever in 1965, building to a strike wave in Victoria and NSW by the end of the decade. Members of the various secondary teachers' unions were at the core of this new surge. From the late 1960s, teachers' primary loyalties shifted from their employers in schools and government to their union, resulting in a breakdown in relationships between teachers and employers. Among factors contributing to the rise of union militancy among teachers was the younger age of teachers overall, the higher qualifications demanded of them, and increasing demand for grassroots involvement in decision making at the level of union branches within schools. Beginning to perceive themselves more clearly as 'unionists' rather than as members of 'professional associations', white-collar workers also took inspiration from the trades and industries.

Finally, the CPA actively supported the proliferation and development of independent shop committees, and CPA members played a role in their growth. Graeme Watson, an ETU shop steward, recalls that 'where there was a Communist Party bloke in the workplace, he had people around him.' CPA members dominated the leaderships of the metal trades unions which were at the forefront of the shop committee movement. CPA officials also dominated the leadership of the NSWBLF. But the role of the CPA should not be exaggerated. A CPA strategy document for the 1980s claimed that party members had 'identified [the penal powers] as major barriers to shop floor activity' in the 1960s and pushed fellow workers 'to experience these barriers ... directly and immediately', and the 'over-award struggle was consciously used to do this.' While individual members undoubtedly played an important role in shopfloor struggles, the party's level of influence was not such that it could organise a mass confrontation between workers and the arbitration system. By 1969, the CPA was smaller than it had been in decades, and its strategists at the time were as surprised as anyone else at the upsurge in social and labour unrest.

Clyde Cameron, as the Australian Labor Party's (ALP) shadow Minister for Employment, perhaps offered the best description of events in a speech to a Sydney industrial relations conference in 1971, emphasising that:

> the shop stewards' movement, the area committees, and other grassroots movements are a fact of life and they are not disposed of merely by referring to them as being 'Commo-led' or as the reaction of dissatisfied British migrants. [They are] expressive of the fact that many workers feel their needs are best satisfied at the workplaces and they are not content to be led by what they regard as the remote control of Lygon Street [Trades Hall].

Indeed, the shop committee movement had far more organic origins than the agitation of the CPA, arising out of the direct interests of workers.[27]

CHAPTER 3
Politics and Ideas

WORKERS' CONTROL AS A CONCEPT

Discussions of radical unionism and workers' control began (or began again) in the late 1960s. Events in Europe and elsewhere, the establishment of the Institute for Workers' Control in the UK, the growing power of shop committees and the virtual destruction of the penal powers had convinced Australian labour and political activists that important changes were occurring in the workers' movement. From 1969, workers' control became a term used to describe various trade union incursions into the traditionally accepted rights and prerogatives of employers, capital and the state. Jack Hutson, a research officer for the AEU, published a lengthy discussion of the tendency in the CPA's intellectual journal, *Australian Left Review*, defining workers' control as:

> the extension of the right of the trade unions particularly in the workshop, through their representatives, to have an effective say in decisions made in respect to such matters as trade unionism, safety, welfare, discipline, wage fixation, appointment of supervisory staff, deployment of labour, technological changes, hiring and firing and access to financial records.

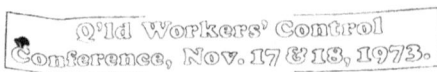
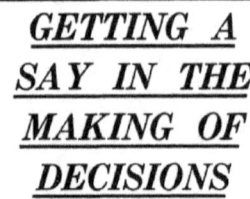

Pamphlet promoting the Queensland Workers'; Control Conference November 1973; (right) CPA newspaper Tribune promotes workers control conference. Tribune 9 July 1969. Photo courtesy Search Foundation.

Hutson and others viewed this as a 'tall order when put against the usually recognised trade union rights.' Workers' control represented a challenge to employers' unilateral right to hire, lay off and dismiss labour, control conditions of work and manage tasks. It threatened the traditionally exclusive right of employers to manage industry without the involvement of workers. It represented not only a more militant unionism, but one that, in many instances, challenged the foundations of the capitalist employment relationship, in which bosses governed and workers obeyed. Denis Freney, a left wing CPA member and prominent teachers' unionist, argued that:

> the trade unions have to change from being generally
> defensive organisations, merely defending the workers'
> economic interests, to an offensive role, challenging
> all aspects of the power, authority and control of the
> employing class.

This shift from defensive to offensive struggle was at the core of this more radical strain in trade union activity, encouraged by industrial relations conditions and social unrest and made possible by the growth in shop committee power and economic conditions, such as full employment.[28]

The movement for workers' control was hotly debated at political forums and conferences. The topic was top of the agenda for the Left Action Conference held over Easter 1969. Trade unionists, academics and, eventually, the CPA also organised a number of conferences. In August 1969, shop stewards across Sydney organised a forum for all union delegates, entitled 'A Case for Democracy in Industry'; held at the Teachers' Auditorium, it was attended by over 200 participants. Advertised in *Tribune*, the forum 'set out to pose questions and seek answers concerning the "right" of employers to decide most questions in their favour.' In their written invitations, stewards were given the example of the recent dismissal of 40 workers at the Email plant in Waterloo, which the company had justified as necessary to avoid closure – before then posting a record profit. This, it was argued, was a clear justification for new struggles to resist sackings and layoffs and to compel employers to 'open the books' so that unions could be involved in finances and governance. In the same month, a public seminar in Melbourne saw unionists, academics and politicians, including Victorian Labor leader Clyde Holding, presenting discussion papers to explain the new discourse of workers' control and ideas of industrial democracy.

The *Australian Left Review* was also an important site for discussion of workers' control. Throughout 1969, contributors, almost all from left wing metal unions, vigorously debated the meaning of the concept. Frank Bollins, an organiser for the Sheet Metal Workers in Sydney and later NSW State President of the AMWU, defined workers' control as existing where 'organised workers of a particular job exercise a decisive influence on the conduct of the industry', which would 'flow from the militant demands of the workers, expressed through mass meeting decisions and implemented by direct negotiations.' Brian Mowbray, a fitter at GM-Holden in SA and chairman of the Combined Shop Stewards' Committee, described it as 'an effective say in the overall planning and running of the factory' which he deemed to be 'synonymous with the recognition of shop committees, and the committees' rights to be involved in planning.' These definitions contributed to a broad understanding of an emergent movement, in which workers were expanding the amount of control they had over industry through their unions and workplace committees.[29]

Some unions and shop committees actively promoted the idea of workers' control. The largest Workers' Control Conference, held in Newcastle over Easter 1973, was co-sponsored by the NSW state branch of FEDFA and the Victorian branch of the AMWU. Unions funded the printing of 50,000 broadsheets, and rank-and-file members distributed them.

Rank and file workers also established bodies concerned with workers' control. In Sydney, for example, a meeting of 18 stewards and rank-and-file unionists established a Western Districts Workers' Control Committee in March 1973. This committee met regularly to discuss ideas and vote on action. Like other organs for workers' control, most of its activities were not concerned with the wholesale subversion of capitalism. Rather, the committee tended to focus on immediate and concrete issues, deciding at their inaugural meeting to generate union support for a community campaign for a pedestrian crossing to be installed in the local suburb, and to pressure the Shop Assistants' Union to tackle shops in the area which were not paying award rates. Overwhelmingly, radical trade unionism began small, with quite concrete demands for higher wages, improved conditions and the right to organise.

Workers' control was principally a tendency toward democracy at the workplace, exercised by shop committees and rank-and-file workers in their own interests or in the interests of communities. Because of this, it was often critical of trade union bureaucracy. Reporting on the previously mentioned Democracy in Industry forum, Pete Thomas, a Miners' Federation organiser and historian, noted that:

CHAPTER 3: POLITICS AND IDEAS 43

CPA newspaper Tribune supports BLF militancy. Tribune 3 June 1970.
Photo courtesy Search Foundation.

a focus of discussion was the issue of 'trade union
bureaucracy' and, linked with this, the relationship of
the shop committee movement to the trade unions
themselves.

Specifically, the independent power of shop committees was perceived as fundamental to the success of workers' control. Indeed, as would be seen in the cases of the NSWBLF, the FIA, the VBEF and elsewhere, union officials could be as repressive and reactionary as employers in their efforts to suppress action at the workplace. Thomas reported that:

> one worker, in asserting the need for 'independence of
> action from trade union bureaucrats', went so far as to say
> that workers' control otherwise could mean 'control by a
> different set of bosses' [in the form of union officials].[30]

Proponents of workers' control emphasised the importance of democratic structures within unions, such as workplace committees, and their need for degrees of independence and autonomy from union officials.

Many on the political left saw worker's control as a movement that could lead to economic and social transformation. They believed that workers could exercise more complete forms of workplace democracy and control, whether through workers' self-management in workplaces or through worker direct ownership. Many looked to state systems like that in Yugoslavia, where government-owned industries were managed through committees of workers and officials. Some looked to the role of workplace occupations and worker takeovers in the early stages of historical revolutions, such as Russia in 1917. At the Democracy in Industry conference, the great majority of those who spoke argued that workers' control could not be envisaged as (or allowed to become) some model to accommodate to the established system of industrial relations. Joe Owens, a CPA member and leading figure in the NSWBLF, described workers' control as 'part of the wider political movement for self-management', not 'restricted to narrow tactics aimed at achieving traditional trade union demands.' Dave Lofthouse, an AMWU shop steward in Brisbane, described it as 'a growing realisation by working people that they must control the mode, purpose and quality of the production process which governs their livelihood', in 'the running of the industry by the people for the benefit of the people.' Trade unions became political organisations in the 1970s in a way not seen before, and some observers were quick to build this into their conceptions of worker's control. Denis Freney, in his 1973 article, argued:

> The right to strike and to form unions are forms of workers' control, limiting the bosses' power ... What is new today is that workers feel the need to go beyond these traditional, partly accepted instances of workers' control to tackle new, formerly unquestioned 'rights' of the boss ... the attempt to impose control over different aspects of the power of the bosses and the ruling class (e.g., the bosses' right to sack ... or what piece of environment to destroy, or what war to fight).[31]

The NSWBLF green bans campaign attacked the traditional right of investors, companies and governments to make decisions about which parts of the environment to preserve and which parts to develop. Writing in *Tribune* that same year, Freney argued that:

> if it begins from this disenchantment at being under the bosses' thumb at work, workers' control is also a tactic by which workers can exercise great control over all the other questions such as pollution control, control over the quality of goods and their prices, control over the destruction of the environment and can also be a means of forcing the boss to give women, blacks and other oppressed groups their rights.[32]

The British Institute for Workers' Control (IWC) was crucial to the development of Australian attitudes. Founded by Tony Topham, Ken

Coates and Michael Barrett-Brown in 1968, the Institute aimed to analyse the trend towards direct encroachment on employer prerogatives by trade unions, including the hundreds of worker occupations, work-ins, worker cooperatives and related developments in Britain throughout the 1970s. The founders of the IWC were eclectic. Distant from the Communist Party of Great Britain, and leading thinkers in the British New Left, each had leanings towards different concepts of socialism. Topham was an admirer of Titoist Yugoslavia who published early works on workers' self-management in that country, and Coates was a member of the International Marxist Group, the British section of the Trotskyist Fourth International. Both Coates and Topham were also tutors in adult education at their respective universities (Coates at Nottingham and Topham at Hull). Through their daily interactions with workers, they were able to establish connections with shop stewards in key industries. The IWC did not merely analyse industrial relations, but also actively advised British shop stewards during workplace occupations and work-ins. After 1974, its members supported the election of a Labour government under Harold Wilson, and Coates and Topham became advisers to Tony Benn. This collaboration between academics, trade unionists and others played an important role in facilitating the development of ideas in a real life context.

The IWC frequently provided literature for an Australian readership. It influenced the establishment of Centres for Workers' Control in Sydney, Newcastle and Melbourne. Workers' Control Conferences, modelled on the British conferences of the same name, were held in Australia from 1969 until the middle of the next decade. The first Australian conference borrowed most of its discussion material from the British monthly journal, *Marxism Today*, concerning the development of workers' control in Britain.

Travel also facilitated the transmission of ideas, as unionists and activists moved between Australia and the UK. Bob Campbell, a prominent Sheet Metal Workers' organiser for Newcastle, was one of several metal unionists to attend a British Workers' Control conference in 1968. Michael Barratt Brown of the IWC addressed a Sydney meeting of metal unionists in March 1972, while Ken Coates himself attended the Newcastle Workers' Control Conference in 1973. The AEU was an important conduit for these ideas from Britain. The Australian AEU was still formally attached to the British union before gaining autonomy in 1968. Its parent organisation included direct strategies for workers' control in its constitution from 1963 and stood for 'worker participation through their trade unions in the direction and management of nationalised industries' as early as 1947.[33]

Sources of inspiration for Australian workers also came from other countries. Hutson emphasised that it was 'near enough to the understanding of what is meant by the demand for workers' control which is being put forward in Europe.' Australian trade union publications regularly reported on European experiments. High-profile occupations in 1973 of a British Triumph factory in Meriden and the LIP watch factory in eastern France, and the conversion of both to workers' cooperatives, were important examples. When LIP declared insolvency, and laid off its workforce, 1,300 dissident workers occupied the factory and reopened it illegally, manufacturing watches without bosses, taking money for wages through sales direct to the public. The *Australian Financial Review* reported with horror:

> The traditional relationship between labour and capital has been called into question ... the Government cannot continue to soft-pedal on the LIP workers [who] have cheerfully shredded the fabric of French commercial, criminal and common law.

As unemployment rose in Australia towards the mid-1970s, articles in the AMWU journal suggested that the appropriation and self-management of a Canadian knitting mill by its employees should be considered a model for Australia. Ron Arnold, a Blacksmiths & Boilermakers' official, returned from Yugoslavia in 1972 to applaud what he described as 'the most remarkable of social experiments', where 'each enterprise has a democratically-elected workers' council on the job which has the complete control of the plant.' AMWU education officers regularly visited Yugoslavia. These foreign experiments created a rich pool of ideas for Australian workers to draw on.[34]

POLITICAL ORGANISATIONS AND IDEAS

Workers' control and radical union actions, where they involved the members of a specific organisation, were generally associated with the far left. Various socialist groups, mostly formed in the 1970s out of the student movement, sold newspapers outside factories and at demonstrations, supported picket lines and even recruited workers. They influenced some disputes, mostly in a small way, and generally in the newly developing white-collar unions. The Socialist Workers' Party, the largest Trotskyist group, declared support for radical union action, but not without a hint of condescension. At its national conference in 1976, green bans were offered as examples of trade union struggles 'of which the revolutionary party must be a part … to win the ear of the militant workers and their respect for our political judgement', because 'there are no organisational shortcuts by which a small party can leap over the unions.'[35]

The influence of anarchist groups was generally negligible because of their low numbers and limited influence, despite the fact that the workers' control movement resonated strongly with anarchist and syndicalist ideas. The view that trade unions might carry the embryos of a system based around direct control of industry by workers was central to anarchist currents from the late 19th century. One history of anarchist ideas captures the point well:

> The most important strand in anarchism has, we argue, always been syndicalism: the view that unions—built through daily struggles, a radically democratic practice, and popular education—are crucial levers of revolution, and can even serve as the nucleus of the free socialist order. Through a revolutionary general strike, based on the occupation of workplaces, working people will be able to take control of production and reorient it toward human need, not profit. Syndicalism envisages a radically democratic unionism as prefiguring the new world.

Workers' control fell quite neatly within older traditions of syndicalism or radical unionism in its rejection of state power and political parties and emphasis on unions and shop committees, the use of political strikes, workplace occupations, work-ins and other forms of radical direct action as means for radical social change. Noam Chomsky, a public intellectual and anarcho-syndicalist, wrote in 1970 that:

> [while] the ideas of revolutionary libertarian socialism, in this sense, have been submerged in the industrial societies of the past half century [where] the dominant ideologies have been those of state socialism and state capitalism… an interesting resurgence [had occurred from the late 1960s, in which] the Workers' Control Movement in England, in particular, has developed into, I think, a remarkably significant force.

Chris Harman, a popular historian and member of the British Socialist Workers Party, also characterised the radical union struggles of the period as syndicalist:

> the largest minority among trade union activists was not formally organised at all. It was made of the many thousands of workers who had basic socialist class commitment, without any fixed political affiliation … If one word had to be used to describe this group it would be 'syndicalist'—except that this implies they had arrived at a finished ideological position, which was far from being the case.[36]

This description can be applied to Australian events in the early 1970s, although on a smaller scale. In both Australia and Britain, labour activists advanced the idea that workers could control and even own their industries, and that they could achieve this through direct action by worker committees and unions. While this is a basic syndicalist view, few would have described themselves as syndicalist, and many remained unaffiliated to political organisations or even specific political or ideological positions.

This was fairly conceded by the CPA, which was historically antagonistic towards anarchism. Jack Hutson admitted that the questions around workers' control and radical union struggles in the late 1960s were also:

> debated at the turn of the century in the controversies as to what was the best way of achieving socialism ... anarchists supported workers' control as an alternative to the state, which they held to be an obstacle to the achievement of socialism, and proposed that it should be exercised through the trade unions as a form of working class self-government.

This was 'supported by the Syndicalists, particularly in France, by the Industrial Workers of the World' and 'by the shop steward and workers' committee movements which developed in Britain during the First World War.' Hutson emphasised that:

> the difference of Marxism ... was that while it agreed on the vital importance of the trade unions it held that the working class required a Marxist political party to help it achieve its objectives.

Where they were active, Australian anarchists criticised the role of the CPA in supporting radical union struggles as opportunistic. A Railway Workers Rank and File Group consisting of anarchists argued at a 1972 Workers' Control Conference that 'anytime a Leninist party proposes workers' control it should be viewed with great suspicion for real workers control would make their organisation redundant.' They argued that democratic control of industry by workers – workers' control – would be problematised by the Marxist or Leninist emphasis on the revolutionary political party and the state as institutions for achieving socialism. The workers' control movement, they said, emphasised self-activity and direct action by workers, prioritising trade unions and shop committees as organisational forms for social change, rather than revolutionary parties.[37]

But the ALP remained by far the most important organisation for the working class overall through the 1970s, particularly the left of the party. Many workers were members of the ALP and saw the party as the way forward. Corey Oakley explains:

> Radicalism in the Labor Party was not simply a matter of rhetoric. ALP branches were a key organising point for the movement against the Vietnam War and, along with students and the unions, provided the backbone of the campaign and many of its activists. The Victorian ALP left, led by Jim Cairns MP, a key figure in the anti-war movement, played a central role. The left's strength was one of the reasons the Moratorium marches were bigger in Victoria than in any other state. Contrast this with the situation today, when 'support' for a campaign from the ALP left or the Greens rarely goes beyond offering official endorsement and perhaps a speaker at a rally or public meeting.[38]

The ALP took different approaches to a more radical trade unionism during the 1970s. While many individual members and representatives supported struggles, the party as a whole effectively ignored ideas about workers' control at the level of policy, leaving the organisation of formal events, reporting and theorising to the CPA.

One critical factor in the development of radical unionism in the period was the development of a split in the Victorian union movement. From 1967, a left wing grouping of the big industrial unions split from the Victorian Trades Hall Council. One of the reasons for the split with Trades Hall was its 'complete ideological bankruptcy which had led to a do nothing, tame cat attitude on wage complaints and other matters of importance to the workers.'[39] The Victorian rebel unions, the major unions in metals, construction and shipping, were dominated by the

CPA, forming a left wing bloc putting pressure on Trades Hall and the ACTU. These unions led the mass strike to free Clarrie O'Shea in 1969 and were critically involved in many of the radical actions of the period. Many workers' control experiences involved these unions, again with the support of the CPA.

An interesting example of a different kind occurred in SA, where the Don Dunstan Labor government took an active interest in some of the ideas expressed by militant unionists, establishing a Unit for Industrial Democracy to research and promote industrial democracy in state industries. The Unit was based on the idea that industrial democracy could be a way to overcome growing conflict between workers and employers; workers' demands for greater degrees of freedom and control in their working lives could be met with appropriate policies. While the Unit was not explicitly opposed to the involvement of independent trade unions in workplace decision making, it was essentially committed to the idea that labour and capital had convergent interests. A 1976 departmental paper commented that industrial democracy 'has gained considerable momentum through the cost to society of disruptive disputes between Labour and Management' and noted that 'prosperity through partnership of labour and capital is beginning to gain a great deal of acceptance in some management circles.'[40] In this respect, it aligned with conservative actors, including large industry groups and the Liberal Party, who were enthusiastic about 'worker participation' schemes instead of workers' control (see Chapter 8). The Unit did not survive beyond the 1970s, because employers tolerated the idea only while it served their own interests. As the strength of unions declined, it became less necessary to accommodate their demands, and worker participation vanished from the industrial landscape in SA.

THE ROLE OF THE COMMUNIST PARTY

Although dwarfed in numbers by the ALP, the CPA was the most important among political parties in its contributions to radical union struggles, both in terms of ideas and in providing leadership on the ground. It was the only far left organisation big enough in size and influence to have a meaningful impact. At the same time, crucially, the Pparty shifted to the left in the late 1960s, making it more receptive to the idea of radical unionism. Large numbers of workers involved in work-ins and other tactics were members of the CPA, while CPA members were particularly active in shop committees and in unions generally. CPA members dominated the leaderships of the major metal unions, the NSWBLF, the Waterside Workers' Federation (WWF), the Seamen's Union and others. These unions were at the forefront in the development of the shop committee movement, because CPA union officials welcomed their development. One CPA publication in 1970 encouraged workers:

> to seek a growing measure of control which encroaches more and more on the sacred domain of the ruling class, [including] control of processes, methods, organisation and supervision of work, including safety on the job, to control over the employer's whole authoritarian discipline system which gives him the 'right' to punish and dismiss workers, the right to hire and fire.

Another document, *A Strategy for the 1980s in the Metal Industry*, evaluated the success of the CPA's industrial strategy in the 1970s in similar terms:

> Has there been an identifiable increase in the power and control of metal workers at the job level? Have 'management prerogatives' been systematically challenged and wound back?

The CPA played an important role in organising and promoting Workers' Control Conferences throughout the early 1970s. Its influence in the major metal unions even gave it the ability to coordinate its own Metal Industry Workers' Control Conference in 1972.[41]

Most significantly, members of the CPA, particularly from within its more libertarian left wing, argued that radical workers' struggles had potential for radical systemic change along socialist lines. As they saw it, the various workplace takeovers and workers' experiments with self-management reflected a latent desire among workers for freedom from employer authority and capitalism itself.

The CPA's attitude contrasts with that of some of the smaller socialist groups because, on the whole, they supported workers' control for its own sake. The CPA's openness to radical new tendencies was probably also partly a result of its own history over the preceding decade. In 1962, the CPA split, with many prominent members leaving to form the Communist Party of Australia (Marxist-Leninist) in response to the Sino-Soviet split. The CPA (M-L) also took issue with the process of democratisation undertaken by Khrushchev in the Soviet Union. Many members remaining in the CPA were interested in democratisation. The CPA opposed the Soviet invasion of Czechoslovakia in 1968 and, in the aftermath, moved in the direction of Eurocommunism. These changes in the CPA had important implications for the workers' control movement in Australia, most notably the BLF. The NSW branch was led by left wing CPA members such as Jack Mundey and Joe Owens. Many of the CPA members who supported workers' control were in a broadly left wing faction of the CPA. Denis Freney, for example, identified as a Trotskyist within the CPA, a position that would have been tantamount to heresy in earlier periods characterised by more rigid ideological adherence to Stalinism. It was in this climate of relative political freedom within the CPA that workers' control took root.

The CPA worked hard to build and support a radical labour movement in Australia. By its own admission, however, the party was responding to a tendency that was already evolving without the guidance or oversight of any political organisation. A document published in 1972, *A Strategy for the 1980s*, conceded that workers would probably have taken many of the actions that they did 'without this strategic objective, or any other to replace it.' This point was reiterated at a National Congress in the same year, which announced that a 'new trend to challenging hitherto accepted "rights" of employers to authoritarian control is shown by the big proportion of strikes against managerial policies.' Workers' Control Conferences were almost always devoted to discussion of workers' control actions *after* they had occurred, rather than to plans or abstract political philosophies. The Newcastle Workers' Control Group justified the need for a 1973 Conference on the grounds that major work-ins had raised questions of capitalist control for other workers. One promotional document read:

> We feel that experiences such as those at Harco, Lanray and South Clifton are increasingly placing the concepts of workers' control and self-management before the Australian labour movement.

At times, the determination of CPA leaders to guide and direct the movement left its members frustrated and oppositional. At a 1972 Workers' Control Conference in Melbourne, a dispute broke out when CPA members could not control the direction of the discussions and walked out. CPA leaders were at times frustrated with the 'larrikinism' of NSWBLF members, who, from the perspective of party leaders, were difficult, unpredictable and lacking in 'seriousness.'

The orientation of the party to workers' control struggles had provoked a major split a year earlier, with a section of the leadership leaving to form the Socialist Party of Australia, repudiating the turn towards what they called the 'discredited path of anarcho-syndicalism.' Union leaders and officials were overrepresented among those who left, perhaps because of their concern that radical workers' committees posed a threat to their authority as union officials. One the most notable was Pat Clancy, secretary of the Building Workers' Industrial Union (BWIU), whose transition from the CPA to the Socialist Party led most BWIU officials to follow suit.[42] The relationship between political organisations and radical trade unionism in Australia during the 1970s is perhaps best captured by a participant, AMWU shop steward John Wallace, who observed:

> the revolutionary party (parties) have endeavoured to change the political consciousness of workers through propaganda, [and have] not basically changed workers who have continually sought more material wealth.

In contrast:

> almost overnight, people ... change dramatically when involved in attempts to encroach upon 'normal' prerogatives of the employers or political authority ... and the more these actions around workers' control continue, the more aware the people involved become.[43]

Through their direct experiences, many workers began to see radical encroachments on the historic rights and prerogatives of their bosses as an almost natural direction for their organisations, based on their own ability to manage their workplaces and control their work and their moral right to do so. For some, the idea that they had no need of a boss was right before their eyes, made evident by the strength and power of their shop committees and through spontaneous acts of self-management.

CHAPTER 4
Radical Unionists at the Workplace

The new radicalism of Australian trade unionists was first apparent in workplace conflicts between workers and their local managers or bosses. On shopfloors, building sites and factory lines, frontline managers and employers scrambled to come to terms with newly emboldened workers and their new forms of organisation. Unions actively sought to chip away at managerial prerogatives in order to to promote greater control by workers over their industrial lives. In 1973, Clyde Cameron, Minister for Employment in the Whitlam government, made the somewhat astonishing proclamation to the conservative Australian Institute of Management (AIM) that 'a better educated workforce and greater industrial democracy are becoming facts of life' and 'action by management in defence of obsolete and inappropriate "prerogatives" can only perpetuate confusion and unrest.'[44]

It must have been rattling for a manager to hear that your prerogatives had become 'obsolete' as a result of trade unions. Nevertheless, a more radical union movement began to express itself through challenges to the historic 'right' of employers to dismiss and lay off workers at their discretion and in a surge of struggles for the right to have closed union shops. Some of these conflicts over hiring and firing exploded in occupations and work-ins. The existence of shop committees resulted in increasing levels of workers' control over health and safety and various aspects of work organisation and job control.

CONTROL OVER HIRING AND FIRING

A large number of disputes centred on hiring and firing. A speaker at the 1973 Workers' Control Conference in Queensland noted that:

> [the] way in which workers' control ideas and tactics can encroach on the powers of the bosses are best shown by examples, most of which have been around the bosses' right to hire and fire.

The focus of shop committees on having a closed shop is one example. Jim Moss, a prominent South Australian unionist, reported in 1973 that:

> [a] large number of industrial disputes are over matters of organisation and particularly over workers resisting joining a union and the unionists and the union insisting that they are members.[45]

Events on one day in March 1969 clearly illustrate the level of workplace conflict over union hire. Some 200 metalworkers attempted to invade the Sydney Industrial Court, then went on strike for two days, over a replacement worker or 'scab.' Meanwhile, all Melbourne trams stopped after a worker, Tom 'the Pest' Pesteranovich, was rostered for work despite having been blacklisted by the union for scabbing. After a number of drivers and conductors were suspended, a mass meeting voted that the strike would continue until suspensions were overturned and the blacklist enforced. Watersiders, who were already on strike on another matter, joined the meeting. Throughout the late 1960s and early 1970s, struggles around union hire fill the pages of the union journals and left wing papers.

Conflicts occurred as unionists sought to secure employment for different groups of workers. A common issue was the obligation to hire unionised apprentices after completion of their apprenticeships. At Australian Newsprint Mills at Boyer in Tasmania, the threat of strike action quickly guaranteed the retention of an apprentice at the end of his

CHAPTER 4: RADICAL UNIONISTS AT THE WORKPLACE   59

apprenticeship. Through the Central Gippsland Trades & Labour Council (T&LC), all unions with apprentices employed by the State Electricity Commission (SEC) in the La Trobe Valley (Victoria) imposed a ban on all contract work in response to the failure of the Commission to keep apprentices after completion of their apprenticeships.

Actions were taken in support of women's right to access employment. The NSWBLF pursued the issue vigorously. In January 1973, for example, 24 NSWBLF members struck at Crow Industries in Sydney, after the foreman refused to employ a woman as a safety officer on the grounds that she was a woman. The strike continued for a week, until she was given the position. In an action that captured some of the mood of the period, women's liberationists targeted AI&S in Port Kembla in 1973, demanding access to employment, staging demonstrations at its gates and even chaining themselves to the fences. The action climaxed with four women activists invading the plant and working for several hours until they were removed by plant security. In the words of participant Janne Reed:

> Our actions were an attack on BHP, not only for jobs for women, but also to attempt to expose their policies and the situation they have created: the poor wages and conditions, the unemployment of women (approx. 6000), the housing shortage, lack of educational facilities for children of working class families and adults wanting to learn English.[46]

These actions marked the beginning of a long campaign against Australian Iron & Steel – the industrial centre of Wollongong and one of the largest employers in the country – for its discrimination against women. It was not until the mid-1980s that the Equal Opportunity and the High Courts found the company guilty for its refusal to employ enough women and for its unfair targeting of women for retrenchment during the downturn of 1982.

Campaigns against companies' use of independent contractors instead of unionised, full-time workers became another way of exercising control over hiring. After a plumbing contractor was killed at a

Dunlop tyre plant in South Melbourne, the shop committee argued that, if there had been shop stewards on the site, the contractors would have been banned or asked to join the union, which had a health and safety committee. In this instance, unions targeted a grey area in federal industrial relations law, because it was beyond the scope of the industrial relations courts to deal with independent contractors. Tony Robins, ETU steward and convenor of the massive Commonwealth Area Committee in the Department of Housing and Construction in Melbourne, recalls that:

> We fought a lot of retrenchments there after 1975 ... They'd have contractors in. We had a maintenance construction workforce ... So we would put bans on the contractors ... The [area] committee was saying we've got to get rid of these contractors, so we started to control what contractors came in.

Bans were also placed on independent contractors in Public Works Departments of Melbourne and Sydney, as well as many of the large industrial enterprises of both Victoria and NSW.

THE RISE OF WORK-INS

By 1971, the post-war manufacturing boom was beginning to decline across manufacturing and related industries. Australia's export markets were squeezed through competition, made worse by the loss of markets in the UK after it joined the European Economic Community in 1969, and the costly American-led war in Vietnam had reduced direct investment from the US. As layoffs and factory closures increased, many workers began resisting, through strikes and occupations, rather than quietly joining the dole queues. Commenting on a survey of metal trades employers, one industrial relations researcher drew the conclusion that:

> the most significant change ... observed between 1969 and 1976 was in respect to terminations ... increasingly

unions have challenged management freedom to
discharge employees arbitrarily ... as a consequence,
most of the companies in the survey had developed some
special procedure to deal with discharge.[47]

Clearly, unions were making successful interventions into the well-established right of employers to sack their employees.

Shipbuilders at the Upper Clyde Shipyards in Scotland staged the world's first work-in to resist the closure of their shipyards by the Conservative Heath government in 1971. Rather than go on strike, rank-and-file shipbuilding unionists decided just to continue to show up for work. Led by the charismatic Jimmy Reid and other delegates, most of whom were members of the Communist Party, they sought simply to show that there was work to be done at the yards. Jimmy Reid said:

Nothing or nobody will come in or go out of the yards
without our permission. The world is witnessing a new
tactic on behalf of the workers.

Ideas of workers' control and industrial democracy were at the heart of the work-in; the action was considered entirely new, different from a more traditional workplace occupation. Reid declared to a joint union committee at the shipyards in 1971:

We are not going to strike. We are not even having a sit-in
strike. We are taking over the yards because we refuse to
accept that faceless men can make these decisions.

This idea – that workers should be involved in economic decision making and policy – was a theme in the various marches and meetings throughout the course of the action.

The tactic at the Upper Clyde Shipyards had mixed results, but the nature of the action electrified the international union movement. For many, it served as a demonstration of democratic workers' self-management. Soon after, work-ins occurred across British industry, including at

Westland Helicopters in Yeovil, Fisher-Bendix in Liverpool and Gardners of Patricroft near Manchester. The work-in tactic situated itself in the radical context of the time as a deliberate political action and a practical tactic for protecting jobs. The term itself reflected this. Occupations were called 'sit-ins' in the 1960s, a term coined by the American New Left and the student movement. In opposition to the Vietnam War, intellectuals and anti-war groups would hold 'teach-ins' at the universities, offering free lectures to educate people about the war. Some activists staged 'die-ins' at military events, feigning violent death and throwing themselves in the way of proceedings to disrupt them. The point of all these actions was to make a political point through direct action.

The first Australian work-in against layoffs occurred in November 1971, when ironworkers and boilermakers wanting to resist proposed retrenchments took control of the Harco Steel factory in Sydney, working for several weeks before they were removed under the Summary Offenses Act. Shopfloor organisation was crucial to the action, and the decision to take over the plant was made through a rank-and-file meeting at a local pub. Mick Tubbs, a CPA member and migrant from the UK, reported on the work-in for *Tribune* and described it as 'spontaneous in the sense that we were trying something new' in reaction to the loss of jobs. Support for the action was offered from as far away as Queensland and Western Australia, while sacked Harco workers visited other workplaces to explain what was done and to develop support in defiance of dismissals. A work-in occurred in the same month at Tulloch, a manufacturer of rolling stock in Sydney. A factory occupation at Johns & Waygood, in Sandringham in Melbourne, won the reinstatement of 25 retrenched workers in an action described by the CPA as 'a splendid lead to the trade union movement on the way to fight mass dismissals.'[48]

Actions to protect union delegates were common. A kind of work-in occurred earlier in 1971, at the medical goods plant Johnson & Johnson, following the targeted dismissal of shop stewards in April. The initial dismissal of the men resulted in 74 maintenance workers walking off, after which the two shop stewards continued work for a further two days, 'escorted through the gates by their fellow unionists', until their arrest.[49] Similar conflict occurred during a wage dispute in the La Trobe Valley power industry in 1973, when metal workers outside the area refused to accept stand-downs consequential on the strike. At the Williamstown Naval Dockyards, the majority of the 70 men who were stood down refused to leave their jobs, informing management that the shop committee would decide such matters and warning the Minister of Defence of a revolt among Commonwealth workers if stand-downs without pay continued. At the North Melbourne Railway Workshop, men who refused to accept stand-downs told managers that the products of their labour belonged to them, but that they would sell the products to management if they wanted, or would otherwise keep them.

Many workplace occupations and work-ins occurred in response to retrenchments. For example, threats by Conzinc Rio Tinto in June 1973 to close its Brisbane Pillar Naco plant provoked swift reaction from workers: a meeting of around 700 decided to stage a sit-in strike, demanding the reinstatement of the 91 dismissed and a withdrawal of dismissal notices to the other 71. The occupation lasted several days, supported by mass meetings and a blockade of the factory gates to avoid removal of equipment. Confronted by the brutal determination of the company, workers were unable to resist the retrenchments.

The likelihood of winning reinstatement diminished as the economy entered recession in 1974, and the focus of work-ins and occupations often turned to improved redundancy terms. Workers at the Evans Deakin shipyards in Wollongong worked-in for six weeks in an attempt to prevent closure of the yards in 1973. Although they eventually accepted redundancy, the action generated widespread publicity. Babcock & Wilcox, a company contracted at Unilever in Balmain (Sydney), issued dismissal notices to 32 AMWU members in January 1975. As a signal of the changed environment (or the new hardness of employers), they had retrenched 800 workers with full severance pay in 1973 but refused to consider severance pay again in 1975. At least 22 workers returned the notices and continued work. In the words of a delegate: 'If Babcock and Wilcox think we're going to join the 270,000 on the dole queue, they've got another think coming.'[50] Redundancy pay became the focus of the campaign, but without success. Clyde Master workers in Bayswater (Melbourne) had more success the following year, achieving generous severance terms after a protracted occupation of the factory over the sacking of 25 workers. AMWU members at Clyde Master had a reputation for opposing any attempts by management to sack them and had established the right for the shop committee to be involved in decision making around changes to labour.

In the automotive industry, wildcat strikes and even riots occurred as workers and managers squared off over job control issues. In August 1971, a worker was dismissed for 'refusal of duty' at the GM-Holden Pagewood plant in Sydney, resulting in an immediate stoppage of all workers in the floor section. At the threat of a strike, plant managers sent a car to retrieve the man so that they could reinstate him.

One worker was jailed for refusing to accept the sack from the Chrysler plant in Tonsley Park (Adelaide) in 1975. After Chrysler retrenched 50 tradesmen, Peter Arend continued to work for a month until his arrest. His actions were endorsed by mass meetings in the press shop and by the shop committee, but bitterly condemned by right wing VBEF officials, with the union state secretary declaring: 'We are fighting a struggle within the union, the struggle is between the VBEF Executive and the rank-and-file committee.'[51] The dismissal of a brewery worker at Tooheys in Sydney's inner west provoked a two-day strike in January 1969. More than 150 workers took strike action at Schweppes in Sydney the following month to reinstate two dismissed workmates, Nick and George. Their demonstration outside the plant carried the slogan 'No Nick, no George—then no work'.

Shop and site committees were important to resisting sackings. However, resistance sometimes occurred spontaneously, without involvement from shop committees. The AEU Commonwealth Council declared in 1969 that it was:

> where workers have been denied timely and adequate leadership on the vital and urgent issues that affect their lives that action of a spontaneous nature inevitably develops ... and that such spontaneous action takes place despite shop committees, not because of them, and in most cases where shop committees do not even exist.[52]

CHAPTER 4: RADICAL UNIONISTS AT THE WORKPLACE

During the 1971 work-in at Tulloch, when the shop committee proposed to a mass meeting that retrenchments be accepted in exchange for settlement terms, rank-and-file workers rejected the proposal and walked back on to the job together with the retrenched men, defying the company and their own shop committee.

A series of work-ins to resist dismissals involved AMWU members at the Sydney Opera House in 1972. Tensions escalated after a fitter was dismissed for the misdemeanour of throwing water over a workmate. The fitter was taken back onto the job in defiance of management and, after three days, was reinstated. Several months later, all workers employed on the revolving stage were dismissed during a dispute over job control. Their immediate response was to refuse dismissals and continue work.

Similar conflicts occurred in the mining industry. A global precedent was set when the first mining industry work-in was staged in South Clifton (NSW) in 1972, inspiring a spate of similar actions. In Tasmania, 10 workers were dismissed from the Renison Bell tin mine for taking strike action in support of a fitter who had been sacked for refusing to carry out tasks outside his trade classification. Assisted by AMWU organisers and the T&LC, all 10 workers refused the sack, quickly winning reinstatement.

NSW miners were particularly active. In late 1974, the Coalex corporation tried to close its Wolgan Valley mine. All the workers tore up their dismissal notices and continued to work for two weeks before they were compelled to accept the closure and move to other Coalex mines. Throughout late 1975, mining companies imposed stand-downs and lockouts to resist the unions' campaign for a log of claims. In late August, miners at Coal Cliff, owned by Conzinc Rio Tinto, refused to accept dismissals and worked for three days at the mine in defiance of the company stand-down orders. The Miners' Federation gave full support to these actions. In a pit-top interview, Bob Kelly, president of the local branch, was asked: 'Do you think miners have a right to put themselves above the law?' to which Kelly replied:

> Which law do you mean? Do you mean the law that's made to suit Conzinc Rio Tinto and other big companies? That's not our law. We uphold moral law. Under moral law,

we have every right to be doing what we are; in fact, under moral law, this mine should be ours anyway.[53]

Coal Cliff was the scene of an earlier work-in. Merv Haberley, a noted union activist, was sacked after he was caught in the shower before knock-off time but continued working the next day as if nothing had happened. The support of unionists at the site and the local branch of the miners' union forced the company to accept his reinstatement. In September, workers at Pelton, near Cessnock, defied stand-downs and embarked on a work-in that produced 1,300 tons of coal before management shut off electricity and removed pit lamps. Other work-ins were thwarted by such management tactics. At a coal mine in Wallarah, for example, one company was quick enough to reverse the trolleys as workers entered the mine to work-in, before shutting the transport system down.

Layoffs and dismissals in the building industry were often triggers for work-ins and acts of self-management. In January 1971, 80 workers at a Brisbane building site went on strike in protest at the dismissal of five of their workmates. A mass meeting demanded that the employer – Concrete Constructions – sack the project manager but reinstate their co-workers.

Retrenchments raised questions about employers' rights. In the words of the BWIU State President for Queensland during the strike:

> Why should bosses claim a divine right to determine whether a worker is to be employed? Is it not time that the workers, at their democratically constituted meetings, have a proper say on this and on who should be the project bosses under whom they have to work?[54]

Questions like these were at the centre of the workers' control movement.

The continued boom conditions in construction meant that workers in the industry were less affected by the downturn. The NSWBLF was particularly militant in its defence of workers who were laid off or who were dismissed for minor disciplinary reasons. A number of actions took place on Sydney building sites. In July 1972, one struggle over dismissals on the Costains Macquarie project prompted the MBA to complain that the union was 'not prepared to concede that the company has the right to employ or dismiss employees as they see fit.' A similar incident took place on a Dillingham site in Martin Place later in 1972. After retrenchment notices were given to four men, all workers on the site refused to accept the layoffs and won a company backdown. In the words of one worker:

> no longer were we prepared to say the boss has got the
> right to sack us as long as he gives us an hour's notice.

The popularity of work-ins in NSW can be seen as an aspect of a broader radicalism. NSWBLF leaders in particular, many of whom were left wing members of the CPA, were attuned to the conversations around workers' control taking place politically.[55]

WORKERS CONTROL HEALTH AND SAFETY

Health and safety issues emerged as a distinct focus in the 1970s, inspired by new quality of life concerns within social activism. The occupational health and safety movement became part of a more general push for public and environmental health, raising trade union consciousness and putting traditional managerial controls over health and safety into doubt. Trade unions have long engaged in campaigns to improve health and safety. However, the idea that rank-and-file workers should directly control risks, rather than merely demanding improvements, emerged distinctively in the early 1970s. It endured until legislative changes in the 1980s transferred control to external bodies and tripartite committees.

Manufacturing had always been fraught with dangers, including frequent exposure to large-scale machinery, heights, poisonous fumes and liquids and extreme heat. Union journals regularly ran articles on industrial hazards and the role of rank-and-file workers in reducing them; the editors of *Link* insisted that 'we can control these hazards at our places of work only through an effective shopfloor organisation.'[56] Throughout manufacturing, control over health and safety was principally achieved through worker health and safety committees, either as functions of shop committees or as independent organs. A typical safety committee was established in 1976 at Brick and Pipe Industries in Scoresby (Melbourne). It consisted of a shop steward from each union and a staff member from each plant. In one action, workers accepted the recommendation of the safety committee and banned any work involving asbestos and barium carbonate, forcing the company to withdraw the materials. Management and the safety committee used information provided by workers to regulate noise levels.

After the catastrophic collapse of Melbourne's Westgate Bridge in 1970, safety committees at the site had broad functions. Danny Gardiner, a rank-and-file FIA member, describes highly organised forms of worker control over safety on the Westgate Bridge. As well as a safety committee, workers formed a 'rescue team' to assist trapped or injured workers, often using specialist skills to access awkward working spaces that paramedics would struggle to reach. In one incident, the rescue team saved a worker's life after he suffered a heart attack. The CPA campaigned explicitly on the idea that workers' control over safety should be a minimum condition at Westgate after its collapse. Gardiner recalls that control was established as a more natural response to the collapse of the bridge and the failure of management systems for protecting workers. Westgate health and safety committees were independent of both management and union leaderships.

Shop committees also took up the issue. In 1976, the shop committee at Ford Broadmeadows (Melbourne) demanded the right to have noise level and toxicity tests conducted, which *Link* celebrated as 'the first time Ford have agreed to encroachments on their "sacred right" to run their plants as they see fit.'[57] Committees clashed with managers in the push to control occupational health and safety (OHS). In many cases, conflict simply arose over the defence of safety personnel. Management at Olex Melbourne dismissed a safety committee nurse in August 1977, only to be forced by strike action to reinstate her. In the same month, workers at International Harvester threatened strike action over the dismissal of a factory cleaner employed to dispose of harmful lead chips, winning his reinstatement. Numerous disputes of this sort occurred

CHAPTER 4: RADICAL UNIONISTS AT THE WORKPLACE

Ford Broadmeadows workers on strike 1973.
Photo courtesy Socialist Alternative.

throughout the mid-1970s as shop committees infringed on traditional management roles.

Conflict frequently arose between workers and specialised company bodies for the regulation of health and safety. Several examples come from Melbourne. Prior to the fatal accident at Dunlop, mentioned earlier in this chapter, union safety officers had resigned in protest against managerial inaction on safety concerns, leaving only company foremen in the safety committee. Workers widely considered this to be a factor in the failure to prevent the accident.

Management at the Bowater-Scott Paper factory in Box Hill in 1978 introduced a series of safety rules which workers thought were more concerned with regulating discipline than ensuring safety. When a worker was dismissed for breaking the rules, all other workers walked out. At arbitration, the company was ordered to reinstate the worker and enter negotiations with the the union to improve regulation of health and safety.

Management at Australian Paper Manufacturers, in Fairfield,

attempted to ban the metal workers' shop steward, Peter Davey, from attending a union-run health and safety course in December 1975, informing him that he could attend company-run courses instead. The ban was overturned through strike action. An AEU delegate at Commonwealth Engineering said:

> the hardest part is to get the boss to move; 'there's no money for him in health and safety.' That's why the demand for workers' own safety committees is on the agenda at so many places.[58]

Workers viewed health and safety as a class issue, not in an abstract sense, but because of their immediate and concrete experiences.

The dangers of the manufacturing industry were rivalled only by those of construction, and the drive for speedy completion of skyscrapers within the building boom brought greater risks. Death by falls increased in line with the increase in development projects; 44 building workers were killed in NSW in the 12 months ending April 1973. Other dangers included deafness and respiratory problems caused by deeper excavation.

Developers' focus on profit at the expense of workers' health, compounded by the ineffectiveness of government regulations, prompted the NSWBLF to intervene directly and impose bans on unsafe practices. For example, members refused to drive free-fall hoists on cranes, because they allowed hooks and loads to fall with gravity in an uncontrolled manner. The ban successfully marginalised the hoists to just a few resistant employers. Bans were also imposed on the practice of dogmen 'riding the hook', which could result in deadly falls. The union waged a concerted campaign throughout 1972 to ensure that two dogmen worked each crane, so that riding the hook would become unnecessary. Resistant employers were black banned, leading to the elimination of the practice by 1973 – despite determined opposition by the MBA. In April 1973, the union threatened to ban any site where equipment was not fitted with necessary noise and dust control devices. By July, 50 places across Sydney had experienced stoppages on the issue, with most employers conceding.

Where employers refused to appoint full-time health and safety officials, direct action could be used to force change. The NSWBLF fought a Civilise the Industry campaign between 1969 and 1970, insisting that all inner-city high-rise jobs had full-time safety officers and full-time first aid officers. Employers successfully resisted until a week-long strike at the Westfield site on William Street in early 1972 won the right to a safety officer. This victory inspired workers at other sites across the city to strike successfully for the same thing. On a number of occasions, safety officers simply worked-in. When PDC Constructions refused to accept a safety officer at a site in Rawson Place, union members simply elected one from their ranks, who worked until he was recognised officially.

Not surprisingly, employers were more opposed to the election of safety officers by workers than they were to the cost of employing the additional staff. A prolonged dispute occurred at the Costains Macquarie site at the corner of Sussex and Liverpool streets because the company objected to the principle of a first aid officer nominated by the union. After the company refused to employ two safety officers, a two-week work-in of the two men led to the involvement of the MBA and the Industrial Commission. The demand for elected safety officers was a key motivation behind the MBA's campaign for deregistration of the NSWBLF; they could see the threat to their right to control labour. The words of Jack Mundey reflect the issue of control:

> we believe we are more competent to control safety
> on projects, to elect people whom we believe can best
> safeguard safety and to elect people who are best fitted to
> be leading hands on the job.[59]

For building employers, the idea that workers would control hiring posed a challenge to their prerogatives.

Worker self-education was fundamental to workers' control over safety issues. The NSWBLF journal regularly contained information about hazards and the relevant regulations, including Greek and Italian translations. At B&D Doors in Melbourne, the so-called 'ethnic shop committee', named for its multicultural and multilingual character, elected a separate safety committee. Its members attended a safety school coordinated by workers and unions. The AMWU spearheaded union education in this area. According to one delegate, it was initially driven by pressure from shop stewards at GM-Holden Elizabeth (Adelaide). They lobbied intensively for 'the union to recognise the need for union education' from 1967.[60] By 1970, the AMWU was coordinating 'health and safety schools … for shop stewards', including the topic of 'intervention at the workplace through union safety committees.'[61] AMWU members also imposed a longstanding ban on lead-based paint at the Eveleigh railway workshops in Sydney, followed by a strike after the Railway Department attempted to break the ban in 1972. Frank Bollins reported that 'shop stewards had themselves gathered information from the union's research centre, Sydney University and the Health Department on the problem of lead poisoning', in order to properly inform their members before they voted for bans. Bollins further explained that, after the strike, workers decided to 'appoint their own on-the-job research officer' and 'won't depend on the department-dominated safety apparatus but will establish their own rank and file safety organisation and set their own safety standards.'[62] Shop committees in the Victorian railways workshops ran their own training on the use of new equipment and other subjects.

The demand for information contributed to the formation of groups that provided advice. The Melbourne Workers' Health Action Group (WHAG), established in 1978, observed in its first publication that 'control of workers' health lies largely with company doctors and managements and the experts they choose to consult', and that 'it is time that the long-suffering workers assumed control of their own health.'[63] The group managed a Workers' Health Resource Centre in Carlton to provide information and technical assistance on regulations and on technical and medical matters, particularly concerning the analysis of materials such as asbestos. Independent Workers' Health Committees established in Sydney and Queensland consisted of rank and file workers, union reps, professionals (such as doctors, lawyers, educators), students and other interested people. Unions, shop committees, individuals and state and Federal governments provided funding. The Queensland Workers' Health Committee based its activities on:

the principles that 1) it is necessary to organise separately from management and 2) workers are in the best position to recognise the dangers they are faced with.[64]

These groups cooperated closely with rank-and-file metal workers. The WHAG, particularly, provided a lot of support in the area of asbestos. The group investigated asbestos-related health problems at a brake and clutch manufacturing plant and ran an investigation that revealed asbestos at the Melbourne City Council Power Station, resulting in black bans. At the Hazelwood Power Station in Victoria's Latrobe Valley, workers black banned suspected asbestos after consultation with experts from the WHAG, demanding regular paid meetings to discuss health and safety on the job and election of their own workers' Health and Safety Officer in each power station or workshop. WHAG supported workers at Granowski Wheelabrators in Bayswater when they placed bans on the removal of asbestos dust for three weeks, forcing the company to provide fully disposable protective clothing and breathing equipment; workers handling the dust also received medical checks at company expense and on company time. The shop committee at Sheraton Fairfield used the WHAG to educate its members about industrial deafness and other issues. An Industrial Health Workers' Group in Sydney distributed literature advising workers how to establish safety committees: 'you will need strong shopfloor support. You will also need organisation' and 'could form into a rank and file health and safety task force' as 'the start of an ongoing health and safety committee.'[65] Workers' control over OHS depended upon the active engagement of rank-and-file workers.

JOB CONTROL

As shop committees and unions at the workplace developed more sophisticated methods of organising, it became more likely that conflict would occur over the control of work itself. That conflict began slowly, with disputes over individual tasks and issues of job control. In some cases, these struggles culminated in work-ins; many others played out on factory floors and building sites in conflicts between rank-and-file workers and frontline managers.

Various conflicts emerged about issues of job control, including work measure, piece work, scientific management techniques that control the individual actions of workers, and methods of completing work. Such struggles had much older traditions. The 1917 General Strike was provoked by the introduction of work measure (intense managerial control over how much work is completed) in the NSW railway workshops. A 1920 article from a Brisbane-based radical workers' education program observed that:

> job control is finding an increasing number of
> advocates … because it points in the same direction as
> the ultimate objective, the ownership and control of
> industry by the workers.

However, even where workers 'do institute job control … set up shop committees' and 'resist speeding-up, prevent overtime and generally secure redress', 'there will still remain a wide gulf between such achievement and the ultimate goal of complete control over industry.'[66]

Similar actions around job control emerged in the 1970s, driven by shop committees and, in some cases, by radical ideas.

Job control (who controls how a job is done) could be considered to be within normal trade union activity. However, disputes over job control pushed beyond conventional boundaries in Australia from the late 1960s. Job control provoked ongoing stoppages in the shipping industry. It was a factor in the severe industrial strife that affected BHP operations from 1969, with construction of a company 'roll on/roll off' terminal delayed for almost a year in 1973–74. Struggles over job control were typically expressed as shop-level conflicts between rank-and-file unionists and managers. Industrial records at AI&S and John Lysaght Steel in Port Kembla are filled with disputes around the issue. After a series of stoppages and bans by fitters at John Lysaght, including heated confrontations with foremen, management called a conference where 'it was made clear regarding the shift maintenance Foreman's responsibility in allocating work, that "common sense" would prevail', and unionists

CHAPTER 4: RADICAL UNIONISTS AT THE WORKPLACE 75

would refrain from interference.[67]

A study by the South Australian Policy Research Group & Political Economy Movement noted that 'absenteeism, labour turnover and industrial disputation reached record levels' in the late 1960s. 'Workers were sick of alienating and inhuman production lines, filthy factories and low wages; they voted with their feet.' At the Cockatoo Docks in Sydney, ongoing disputes occurred throughout 1975 because of job dissatisfaction. Unionists at the Everhot stove manufacturing plant in Port Melbourne banned further work in June 1975, simply because conditions of work were terrible. In many railway workshops, the powerful shop committee network engaged in an ongoing confrontation over work quality. For example, the shop committee at the Ballarat North Railway Workshops rebelled over the stripping of fixed wheel wagons, requesting that the entire workshop be renovated and remodelled to improve the quality of work and reduce employee discontent.

The Central Industrial Secretariat, a sort of super-federation of such employer associations as the Metal Trades Industry Association and the Chamber of Manufacturers, took the view in 1974 that:

> the most fundamental area ... in which industry is facing social challenges concerning its relationship with its employees, is in respect of the nature of work itself.

The Secretariat attributed this to 'conflict between individual fulfilment and the goals of maximisation of productivity' and the 'alleged dehumanisation of work.'[68]

During a strike over conditions at GM-Holden Elizabeth in 1970, VBEF officials told workers to go back to work; the officials were 'physically chased out of the plant and anything movable was thrown at them.' Managers and plant foremen were also thrown out. The involvement of AEU members in the incident prompted intervention from the AEU State Secretary, who reported:

> I attended the Elizabeth plant at approximately 9.50a.m. and advised the G.M.H management that I was very

> concerned that the situation had got out of control of the people handling it … I felt that the situation was such that the A.E.U were being pulled into a problem which the people concerned could not control.

The union members at the plant stressed the 'need for control over the production line' and 'arrogance shown by production foremen.' Workers won concessions, including the right to extended breaks and a measure of control over the speed of the production line, with the AEU State Secretary applauding the fact that 'these body shop workers of all the 25,000 employees in G.M.H. are the first to have a say in the speed of production.'[69]

Workers at the Ford Broadmeadows (Melbourne) plant in 1973 responded even more physically, destroying property and turning a fire hose on management offices. As at GMH, AEU officials reported that workers' grievances were centred around the 'speed of the line, the pressure upon the workers on the line, and the intolerable manner of Company supervision towards workers on the line.' Although he avoided being chased out of the plant, the AEU State Secretary expressed regret for earlier telling AEU members to accept a 5 percent wage, believing that this had been a cause of the riot. He admitted he:

> did not take into account how explosive was the hatred of the Ford Company by car assembly plant workers … almost driven to madness by the pressure of the line … only too ready to grab the first opportunity to fight the company.

As a result of the Ford strike, the Arbitration Commission forced a discussion on the issue of alienation at work. A prominent rank-and-file AEU member involved in the strike, Sol Marks, remarked that he 'was happy with the ruling on alienation because we, the workers, were alienated between each other and with the product.'[70]

This attitude of workers towards employment was an important feature of the radical struggle during that period. Ron Carli, a production

CHAPTER 4: RADICAL UNIONISTS AT THE WORKPLACE 77

worker, remembers that workers struck for no clear reason – they were so infuriated by the tedium and the everyday repression of their work. He recalls:

> it's just impossible to articulate; *why are we on strike?* ... It's the way you're being treated, the attitude of some of the managers, the way things are. And you just can't put an actual reason for it, but you're just so dissatisfied.

Sol Marks made similar remarks about a Ford strike in Geelong in 1969, where workers 'did not know exactly what they were striking about.'[71] Beyond having some control over the speed of production – limited, of course, by the company's profit incentive – these workers were unable to establish control over the details of their jobs. As factory line workers, they were significantly constrained by the factory line itself. In the words of one worker:

> there is little choice about the work: what is done is done for others, the way they want it, at the quality and at the rate they set. For an assembler, there's no room for creativity.[72]

In the absence of opportunity to wage more subtle job control struggles and to win gains in the area, strikes and sabotage became more attractive.

Scientific management schemes (in which every action and movement of the worker was prescribed and measured) were introduced widely in the late 1940s and were resisted in many trades. Resistance intensified in the 1970s. Disputes over time and motion studies appear throughout *Link*. Many of the actions were local and spontaneous. At Tulloch Engineering, where the 1971 work-in occurred, the use of timecards by foremen was successfully banned by workers immediately after their introduction. A work standardisation scheme at Box Hill Engineering, in which workers were required to maximise their efficiency by walking only along coloured lines within the plant, was abandoned after engineers responded with ridicule: physically balancing on the lines, or getting 'lost' by deliberately taking wrong lines. These workers were highly skilled toolmakers from the North of Italy, some of whom had experienced the explosive factory occupations during the Hot Autumn there.

In general, the existence of shop committees was instrumental in successful resistance to scientific management. Even later into the decade, as shop committees declined in number and influence, struggles over scientific management occurred where committees existed. At Sydney Cooke, a large factory making wire spools in Brunswick (Melbourne), 50 maintenance workers took immediate strike action when a foreman put up a bell to regulate the workday, successfully having it removed.

The IWC argued that productivity incentives were used 'to destroy workers' controls at the shopfloor ... and to establish greater managerial authority over the use of labour', necessitating 'a coherent and co-ordinated counter-strategy' by unions.[73] In Australia, skilled AEU members led the anti-incentives movement, particularly in Newcastle, generally through direct action. Job organisation was crucial to the resistance of incentive schemes. At Gadsden's engineering in Melbourne, 400 metal workers struck to remove an unpopular bonus scheme measuring worker output, under which supervisors would assess the workers who would be paid according to their 'value to the company.' Strikes occurred among AMWU members at the large Rainsfords engineering plant in Adelaide throughout 1975 and 1976 over a company merit scheme.

In contrast to the explosive reactions of 'unskilled' production workers in vehicle manufacturing, more organised disputes over control occurred between skilled vehicle inspectors and company management. In 1972, vehicle inspectors at GM-Holden in Melbourne struck over a shortage of inspection staff which saw the foremen signing the documents without inspection. Fourteen AMWU members struck to demand more inspectors and proper quality safeguards. This was not long after Ralph Nader published his best-selling exposé of multinational car manufacturers, *Unsafe at any Speed*, detailing their efforts to cut costs on safety in pursuit of profit. While it is unclear whether or not workers were aware of the book, it did target GM specifically and resulted in the passage of seatbelt laws across the US.

CHAPTER 4: RADICAL UNIONISTS AT THE WORKPLACE

In late January 1973, inspectors at Ford Broadmeadows in Melbourne struck again, this time for the right to control temperature levels. They claimed that their instruments and gauges required a standard temperature, and that fluctuations made control more difficult. Two shop stewards were dismissed for supporting inspectors who refused to accept a new system of inspecting seatbelts. In response, 250 members of the Amalgamated Metal Workers and Shipwrights' Union (AMWSU) obstructed production lines to demand their reinstatement. Ron Poole described how workers 'immediately formed barriers to prevent production from going ahead' and even 'pushed vehicles back onto the production line and jostled with company representatives.' The VBEF members informed managers that, if their pay was deducted because of the stoppage, they would 'overturn vehicles, use hammers, use forklifts to push over pallets of engines and so on.' Poole described this as 'an on-the-job response not seen before at Broadmeadows.' The stewards were reinstated after three hours, and the old method of seatbelt inspection was reintroduced according to the inspectors' demands.[74]

Struggles around controlling operations were not limited to mass manufacturing. In 1976, a dispute occurred at IMCO Containers in Ferntree Gully (outer Melbourne) over worker demands for improvements to the rostering system. When management attempted to dismiss the AMWU shop steward, he refused to accept dismissal, supported by other unionised workers. When the workers occupied the factory, the company gave in. *Link* reported that, in response to workers' demands, 'the bosses McCann and Bennet would cry, "You are trying to run the Factory".'

In a larger scale action the same year, a thousand workers forced the giant multinational Pilbara iron ore company, Hamersley Iron, to allow workers to have a say in running the company's operations. AMWU members initiated the dispute, requesting changes to job allocation under a work plan devised by the union. Rejection of the proposals by Hamersley Iron provoked a three-week strike, paralysing the industry, with 21 iron ore carriers lined up for 32 kilometres outside Dampier Harbour waiting for loading to recommence. In a significant concession, the company agreed to the establishment of a new railway workshop at Paraburdoo with union involvement. Workplace organisation was instrumental in the success of both the IMCO and Hamersley cases; the Hamersley campaign was coordinated by a tightly organised AMWU strike committee.

At the Shell Oil refinery at Clyde on the Parramatta River (NSW), FEDFA members challenged company management on issues of control over work in a series of dramatic shop floor battles between 1974 and 1978. The introduction of new technology was a catalyst for the dispute, with workers refusing to use new equipment until their claims for higher pay were met. At the climax of the dispute, workers refused to accept dismissal and continued work under self-management until they were forced to abandon the action by the intervention of the NSW Arbitration Commission. Because of their industrial position and their specialised knowledge about the job, FEDFA drivers, trained in operating the machinery, had unique access to control over the production process. They were supported by union officials, but their actions were initiatives of the rank and file, as is clear from the remarks of a shop steward:

> we had discussions about what we could do instead of striking; everybody's against striking despite what the newspapers print, and we looked at ways of controlling production.[75]

Workers sought to establish independent control over work because of a desire for freedom from authority and increased control over their lives. In the words of AMWU organiser Frank Cherry, issues of authority were:

> in many cases more important than wage claims; workers spend eight hours each day at work, and there is no reason why they should be subject to indignities for this period.

This probably captures the motivations of most workers involved in job control struggles. The desire to control work springs from deeply human impulses. Carter L. Goodrich, in his extensive studies of British shop stewards in the 1910s, argued that:

the roots and beginnings of the control demand are in the felt irksomeness of the present system of control, not in a conscious desire for a new field of activity.

He observed that 'control is no "simple central objective", no one clear-cut thing which people either know they want or know they don't want.' Instead, it is a complicated set of urges, perhaps unified by a basic fact of human nature: people tend to prefer freedom over domination.[76]

CHAPTER 5
Work Without Bosses

From the more low-level stirrings of job control struggles and conflicts around hiring and firing came more serious challenges to the established rights of bosses and employers to manage industry. Actions to resist sackings, struggles over job control, and the growing power of shop committees led to actions in which workers 'dismissed' their managers and worked without bosses. These actions were often short lived, but they provoked repression from the bosses. While some workers involved in work-ins wanted simply to stop layoffs or to win other gains, some saw such actions as more significant – the desire for lasting self-management. For these workers, the work-in expressed an urge for freedom from the domination of managers and employers and from exploitation of their labour for the purposes of private profit.

HARCO

The work-in at Harco Steel in Sydney resulted in a prolonged period of workers' self-management that seemed to represent more than just an opposition to proposed sackings. Resisting the sackings, boilermakers and ironworkers took full control of the factory for more than four weeks.

Rumours of retrenchments had been circulating among Harco workers in the lead up to the work-in. When several workers were served retrenchment notices, the decision to reject the notices and show up for work anyway was made the same night in the local pub. They knew that there were plenty of orders and that the attempted sackings were profit-driven. In the words of one worker, they could see that 'there was work to be done, and that it was the capitalists who did not want it done because they could not profit from it.' They decided to continue to show up for work in defiance of the company. Jack Sponberg, a boilermakers' delegate, captured the mood:

> You know what has to be done and you have the initiative; you don't have to wait for the boss to tell you what needs doing ... There is no blueprint for this tactic—you have to find answers as you go along.

One foreman at the plant, who was particularly disliked by the workers, was quickly 'sacked' by a shopfloor meeting. His attempts to give workers instructions were thereafter ignored. In his place, workers elected their own foreman from among themselves. For four weeks, Harco self-managed their workplace, without bosses. Decisions were made by workplace meetings. Two participating workers wrote in *Tribune* that Harco workers:

> had to decide what form of discipline should exist in place of the employer's form of discipline ... The workers decided that only discipline imposed by a majority at a general meeting would reflect their aspirations. Collective self-discipline through the democratic process was adopted and applied.[77]

Finally, after scratching their heads for a month, Harco management called the police. The subsequent threat of heavy fines and jail terms was enough to break the resolve of the workers and end the action. By this stage, however, they had set a powerful example for workers elsewhere and, as far as employers were concerned, a dangerous precedent.

Why were the Harco workers able to take such a major step? Firstly, they were skilled metalworkers who were capable of continuing work without instruction and without control by managers or machines. Perhaps more importantly, their capacity to self-manage their enterprise was assisted by their high levels of discipline and self-organisation. This was largely due to the shop committee, cultivated in the course of previous industrial struggles during which workers – as Mick Tubbs described it – 'gained real experience in their own organisational capacities and started to understand what the class struggle was all about.' During a strike over wages earlier in 1971, for example, ordinary rank and file workers helped with many tasks, showing high levels of cooperation and self-organisation.[78]

The action at Harco revealed some contradictions within the union. The right wing officials of the FIA not only failed to support the work-in; they actively supported management in involving police. In exchange for the cooperation of union officials, fines were levied at individual workers rather than at the union. The complacency and antipathy of union officials in this case may indirectly have helped to encourage self-management at Harco, because union members there were simply used to doing things for themselves.

The Harco work-in inspired other actions. A few weeks later, members of the FIA and Blacksmiths & Boilermakers' Society dismissed their supervisors at Byrne & Thomas Installations in Sydney and worked under self-management to complete outstanding contracts. In this case, the action evolved out of a wage claim by the shopfloor committee, which the company denied on grounds that it was performing poorly and could not afford it. When the company further announced that the installations section of the company might be closed down, the workers took over the factory, working for almost two weeks with no supervision. In the words of one worker:

> We showed that supervision isn't needed ... We did the work in the same way we knew to be best. It was done more smoothly and with better cooperation all round.

Don Currie, chair of the committee elected to coordinated the action, further illustrates this: 'We showed how work can be done, and done better, without standover or pushing or interference from above.'[79] The outcome of this action was starkly different to the Harco result. Rather than sacking workers and contacting police, Byrne & Thomas granted participating workers a pay rise and a permanent degree of freedom from their company-appointed supervisors.

Members of the CPA were involved in actions at both Harco and Byrne & Thomas, and socialist ideas circulated among workers at both workplaces. More importantly, the radical implications of these actions were not lost on the people – workers and employers – who observed them. *Tribune* suggested: 'that the work was done so well by the workers was acutely embarrassing to Byrne & Thomas and was disturbing to other employers.'[80] The alarm with which employer associations reacted to workers' control in subsequent years showed the idea that workers could run their workplaces without owners and managers to be a dangerous one.

THE SYDNEY OPERA HOUSE

After a spate of strikes and smaller work-ins, the final stages of construction at the Sydney Opera House were completed by AMWU and BLF members without managers. The theatres and revolving stages of the Sydney Opera House had been sites of bitter industrial conflict from the commencement of their construction in early 1971. By the start of the 1972, three foremen had been forced to leave because of conflict with unionists.

One continuing issue was wages. The company, McNamee Industries, had priced the contract in 1969, prior to the surge in wage increases that followed the demise of the penal powers. Workers' response to what they perceived as excessive company bureaucracy also caused almost constant, low-level strike action. McNamee regularly stopped work to manage small budgetary decisions. As a result, as many as two or three stoppages would occur daily, with workers striking to recover wages for lost time. A few months prior to the work-in on the revolving stage, a worker was kept on the job by his comrades after he was dismissed for a minor misdemeanour. John Wallace and Joe Owens saw this as 'a big step

CHAPTER 5: WORK WITHOUT BOSSES

forward in a new and virtually unknown tactic to the men' and 'a turning point in the nature of the battles to come.' They observed:

> The member first defied the foreman, then the engineer and finally, the site superintendent, to take him off the job … For three days the sacked man was smuggled on and off the job – not actually working on the job after the first day, but in hiding, turning up for meal breaks, participating in meetings with the fitters and being seen but unreachable by management and site security police during this time.

Eventually, the company capitulated and reinstated the man. Finally, after a dispute over work allocation, McNamee attempted to dismiss its entire workforce of around 45 men. In response, these workers simply continued working the next day, refusing to recognise site foremen and security:

> As their employees gradually entered the job meeting going past the serious faced trouble-shooter (a Mr. Swindell from McNamee) and his henchman, with smiles and light-hearted rejoinders, the management pickets (a reversal of the usual roles!) must have realised that authority was slipping from their grasp.

After the smashing open of the padlocked equipment boxes:

> The enthusiasm was unbelievable and work processed at a rate unknown on the job. The absence of imposed discipline, together with the camaraderie created a harmony on that first day that surpassed anyone's expectations … It was like being released from prison after years of hard labour. Boredom and the hatred of oppression were gone, leaving an exhilarated feeling of release. Even the most menial tasks were performed with enthusiasm.

In the end, Opera House workers self-managed their site from early April to mid-May. In the end, all workers were reinstated, paid in full the wages they were owed from the period without managers, given power to elect their supervisors, and granted a 35-hour working week, an ongoing demand of the AMWU and BLF.[81]

OTHER INDUSTRIES

Wages claims, disciplinary issues and dismissals were often the issues that sparked work-ins or other innovative actions. During the building of a new hospital in Perth in 1973, Trident Construction blocked union officials from accessing the site, twice having them removed by police. The workers then set up a union site committee. When their shop steward was dismissed days later, workers called an indefinite strike and were locked out. In a unexpected turn, workers then approached the Public Works Department and offered to build the hospital themselves, with their own elected supervisors and with quality control and inspection by the department. Dave Price, the sacked shop steward, perhaps capturing the larrikinism of the times, ridiculed the quality of the company's project management by remarking that 'we couldn't do it any worse than Trident.'[82] While the workers' plans never materialised, they show the level of worker initiative and self-organisation during the period.

At Fibre Containers in Box Hill (Melbourne), a particularly authoritarian supervisor was 'sacked' by maintenance workers. His final infraction was trying to continue to operate the plant during a national stoppage of metal workers. After being 'sacked', he was reportedly ignored so systematically by the workers at the plant that the company had little choice but to dismiss him after three weeks of humiliation.

Declining employment sparked a major strike in Newcastle in April 1973. When the Public Works Department retrenched 30 construction workers, 108 walked off in protest, striking for eight weeks. Five-and-a-half weeks into the strike, a group of workers staged an innovative type of work-in. Trade unions in Newcastle had been lobbying for the expansion of the Newcastle dockyards. The striking men worked-in by demolishing a wharf, a necessary step for construction of a new dock. They worked a 35-hour week and recorded their hours – and billed the Public Works Department for their wages. Whether or not they succeeded remains unclear, but the action received broad support across NSW and was a point of discussion among proponents of workers' control. The strike itself was sustained through donations, mostly from the 1973 Newcastle Workers' Control Conference and the NSWBLF. At the conference, delegates reflected on the significance of such actions for economic decision making and democracy. Unions, they argued, should have a role in economic planning. Rather than leaving these decisions to governments, private companies and investors, working people should be significantly involved in the decisions affecting their working lives and their communities. This sort of direct action by Public Works employees could be a way to achieve it.[83]

THE BLF

The democratically elected leadership of the NSWBLF was committed to expanding and enhancing internal union democracy, reducing the distinction between leaders and members and transferring power to the rank and file. The NSWBLF introduced limited tenure for union officials, temporary organisers, the opening of executive meetings to all members, the tying of officials' wages to the BLF award and the non-payment of officials' wages during strikes. While these policies went well beyond those of other militant unions during the period, some of them were symptomatic of the broader militant turn. Mass stopwork meetings became important decision-making tools. In parallel to the shop committees in manufacturing, the NSWBLF also emphasised job-site autonomy. The site-level decision making of the construction industry was more fluid than formalised shop committees within manufacturing.

The NSWBLF's resistance to sackings was at the core of a number of work-ins throughout Sydney. In February 1972, at the Lanray project undertaken by Brisbane-based Concrete Constructions, 50 labourers were dismissed after striking over a pay claim. Despite being told not to return to the site, all 50 workers showed up the next day and 'sacked' all foremen on the site, leaving only a manager to 'facilitate payment.' Within an hour,

labourers had elected five foremen from among their number, as well as an extra first aid attendant. The company director, Ted Cooper, arrived on site dismayed and contacted the union office, agreeing to renegotiate the original pay claim in the workers' favour. However, when the company insisted that a condition of reinstating all workers and increasing wages was the reinstatement of the company's foremen, workers threatened to strike again. The outcome of this action remains unclear. A union Dispute Book notes that, months after the initial action, workers were threatening

CHAPTER 5: WORK WITHOUT BOSSES

BLF and supporters demonstration Sydney October 1973. Tribune 30 October 1973. Photo courtesy Search Foundation.

to strike if the foremen were reinstated, suggesting that some degree of self-management may have endured for a considerable period.

Union radicalism escalated the following year, when construction of the Wyong Plaza in NSW was held up for several days by an occupation. When a NSWBLF member was sacked for absenteeism, other unionists supported his refusal to accept the sack; all workers were then sacked. Immediately, a mass meeting voted to work-in. No sooner had they elected foremen, than 60 police officers cordoned the site off and arrested an organiser, Tony O'Beirne, and six workers for trespassing. Seven workers broke through the cordon and climbed a crane, occupying the jib for three days. Workers and community members provided support by throwing them food and supplies. When workers attempted to hold a mass meeting on the site, a further two dozen were arrested. Humiliated by the crane occupation, police began throwing rocks and bricks at the occupying workers. When one worker was badly injured by a rock and had to be lowered on a stretcher, the police withdrew, and the offending officer resigned.

With the police gone, the workers were able to take full control of the site and begin work under self-management. They declared the site to be under the ownership of 'Building Workers Pty. Ltd.' *Tribune* reported:

> The 67 building workers on the job have sacked [the management], and taken over in the name of their own 'company.' A meeting of workers and residents next Monday night will decide what building they want constructed on the site.[84]

Proposals to convert the site to a hospital were rejected at the meeting; a *Tribune* reporter wrote that this was a result of the deliberate stacking of the meeting by local business owners. Workers soon agreed on the demand that a new contractor for the project be found, and that permanent workers' control be introduced for the remainder of the job. Within a month, their demands had been met. With a new contractor, the workers' committee had rights to hire and fire, elect all leading hands, supervisors and foremen, and be consulted on major construction decisions. Workers received no pay for their month-long occupation, but levies of NSWBLF and FEDFA members, as well as individual job sites, supported them financially.

MINING AND ENERGY

Remarkable experiments with self-management and workers' control occurred in the energy sector. When Australian manufacturing entered a period of critical decline from the early 1970s, coal mining was already in its long boom. By the end of the 1970s, it had become a leading export. Australia's output of raw black coal doubled over the course of the 1970s, from 50 to 90 million tons. Total employment in these mines grew by over one-third between 1970 and 1980. However, despite these figures, mine closures were common. The enormous wealth of mining corporations, as well as the high profitability of most operations, meant that companies would often simply close down a mine and quickly move on to another venture if sufficient profit could not be extracted. This obviously caused friction between mining companies and the militant Miners' Federation.

The first recorded Australian coalmine occupation, or 'staydown', followed a lockout in Korumburra in 1936. In the following decades, staydowns were an occasional feature of industrial action among miners in south Queensland and northern NSW. Perhaps the most notable staydown occurred at the Rosewood colliery in south Queensland in December 1968. To oppose retrenchments, workers occupied the mine for five days, supported by community donations and food from the Women's Auxiliary; they were even treated to an underground concert by a local band.

In 1972, the staydown tactic developed into work-ins. Faced with retrenchments and mine closure, coalminers at South Clifton (NSW south coast) took over and ran their coal mine for three days, a world first. The mine had been under public ownership until it became profitable enough for privatisation in the late 1940s. By 1972, it was run by Clutha Development, wholly owned by US steel tycoon Daniel K. Ludwig. After Clutha was pushed out of the Italian market by a competitor, it moved to close South Clifton. In response to this and other mine closures, the Miners' Federation launched a campaign for national planning in the industry as an alternative to the corporate free-for-all. When Clutha attempted to close the mine in April 1972, the workers, inspired in particular by the Upper Clydeside work-in, staged their own work-in. The local lodge (union branch) president told one journalist, 'I told Clutha's Mr. Van Brink that, if Clutha went ahead with these mine closures, he would have another Upper Clyde on his hands.'

Clutha officially dismissed all the workers on a Friday. On Monday, all workers turned up for work as usual and, with officials from five unions at the pit top, work resumed. Probably in response to the comments of the local Miners' Federation branch, Clutha management had attempted to avoid a work-in or a staydown by turning off power to the mine and padlocking the switchbox. Workers hacksawed it open, despite a supervisor's threats to call the police. One worker said: 'We can't let legalism strangle us.' In another diversion, supervisors offered to pay workers to carry out tasks that were required to shut the mine down. The miners paid them little mind, resuming coal production. In three days, they extracted almost a thousand tons of coal. On the fourth day, Clutha offered to withdraw all dismissals and find work for all workers at the mine until they could be transferred to other mines in the area. In the absence of a clear alternative, the miners settled.[85]

The work-in at South Clifton electrified unionists in the mining industry and beyond. At Port Kembla, the Firemen & Deckhands Union banned coal export ships, including one which was to load the last of the South Clifton coal, until the miners said to lift it. Upon learning that Clutha was withholding its coal trucks from the work-in, a group of local workers volunteered the use of their own trucks. The Clifton hotel gave a free keg of beer to the miners at the end of their first shift. The local Labour Council gave full endorsement, while the Queensland T&LC resolved that the action 'challenges the "God-given" right to hire and fire' and 'adds a new dimension to the trade union movement.' Mineworkers even erected a sign at South Clifton pit top, renaming it the 'Eureka' mine, and other signs opposed corporate capitalism, including one that read: 'Who owns Australia?'[86]

South Clifton inspired similar actions across the industry. Around a month later, workers at another Clutha-owned coal mine in western NSW, Western Main, worked-in to resist mine closure until the company broke the action by cutting off power to the site. In October 1973, management of a Huntley coalmine owned by a subsidiary of the NSW Electricity Commission introduced a 'no work until further notice' order after a series of clashes between rank-and-file workers and supervisors culminated in dismissals and discipline issues. In response, all workers showed up, dismissed their managers and worked under self-management until management cut off the power. Undeterred, workers continued working at the pit top until work ran out, when they took traditional strike action. Workers were galvanised by their experience of self-management; in the words of one worker involved:

> We don't need any bosses; we can produce coal better without them. Give us our own CMU [Combining Mining Unions] members, and that's all we need.

After two weeks, workers won reinstatement of all dismissed men and improved bonus pay. When management tried to include the condition that workers 'comply with reasonable instruction', one mineworker replied: 'In our book, a "reasonable instruction" is one that we comply with; if we don't comply with it, then it's an unreasonable instruction.'[87]

Sometimes, workers chose self-management during strikes as a means of minimising public disruption. In the NSW electricity sector, the Electricity Commission Combined Union Delegates' Organisation (ECCUDO) was organised in the course of a major strike over the 35-hour week in 1973. Power workers elected delegates from several unions to shopfloor committees. It was, from the start, an exclusively rank-and-file organisation. During a later strike, in January 1975, ECCUDO demanded the right to negotiate award claims in place of union officials, rejecting attempts by the NSW Labour Council and officials of all 23 unions in the power industry (other than the AMWSU and FEDFA) to end the strike. Jack McBean, an industrial officer at the Labour Council sympathetic to ECCUDO, commented that this strike was 'not about wages and conditions' but about ECCUDO 'trying to take the right of their trade unions to negotiate for them.'[88]

During the 1973 strike, two members of ECCUDO at each power station organised to maintain operation of power stations in defiance of their managers, in order to continue the provision of power to the public. The State Liberal government, led by Robert Askin, reacted by restricting power supplies, forcing power outages which resulted in stand-downs in other industries. In response, ECCUDO and the AMWU took out newspaper advertisements instructing workers on the way to reconnect power at their workplaces. This sparked a string of actions by workers, reconnecting power and demanding work. Before long, they forced the lifting of power restrictions. *Tribune* remarked:

> This outstanding example of workers' control—showing that workers can take over and run a complex industry—contrasts sharply with the irresponsibility of the Askin Government.

The *Sydney Morning Herald* reacted with horror, decrying the fact that 'workers in the power industry are now controlling, and limiting, Sydney's peak-power supply' and that there was 'talk of extending workers' control to other fields':

> rail workers have been urged to run train services themselves during strikes 'thus giving the workers they were taking to work an example of what they could do.'

Similar events unfolded during a major, unsuccessful power strike in 1975. ECCUDO members took over the Cockle Creek power station in Newcastle, after 'management did not provide staff labour to keep the station operative, as in past strikes, and hinted they might close it down.' According to one reporter: 'The workers will decide what power is produced and where it goes.'[89] ECCUDO maintained this level of self-organisation and interest in self-management until its decline later in the decade.

At the massive ICI Botany (Sydney) chemical plant, more than 1,000 workers went on strike for over six weeks in March 1973. The strike committee provided chemicals to the public as needed. In the words of *Tribune*: 'insofar as the workers are determining who needs and gets what chemicals from ICI, they are exercising a form of workers' control.'

Some of the most dramatic incidents of this type occurred during a major strike over renewal of the Oil Industry Award between July and August 1972. To supply fuel for essential services, oil workers, organised largely by the AMWU and FIA, took over key aspects of oil distribution.

According to *Tribune,* at Newcastle, 'allocation of petrol for essential needs ... was entirely in the hands of the workers on strike.' A strike committee, consisting of 15 fitters and two ironworkers, allocated fuel supplies to outlets at central locations throughout the city and distributed vouchers to the public, authorised by the combined oil unions. Even Newcastle police were forced to request supplies 'for police to get to and from their homes', with the committee deciding that 'the police should have to travel on a pool system, like everyone else.'[90]

A complex system of controls was developed by workers throughout the state during this strike. Upon learning that some petrol stations were using the strike as a excuse to raise prices and sell black market petrol, unions threatened to ban indefinitely any petrol station found doing so. At Wollongong, workers banned all supplies leaving the Mobil depot; in response to public protest, they requested that the companies release supplies from the *BP Endeavour,* berthed at Port Kembla, for essential services. When the companies vacillated, the unions threatened to take full control of the *BP Endeavour* in order to ensure supplies. The South Coast Labour Council secretary (in what was something of a refrain by this stage) said: 'We told them that they would have a new South Clifton on their hands.' Government was particularly alarmed by this action. The Minister for Primary Industries denounced it as 'a straight out blackmail attempt by the union movement to act de facto as the alternative government.'[91]

Workers' control during the oil strike was overwhelmingly rank and file. At BP Crib Point in Westernport Bay (Victoria), seamen and refinery unionists took over entire sections of their operations in 1973 in support of those on strike. When a tanker arrived, seamen would ascertain the intended cargo and destination. They would contact shop stewards from the refinery and decide, jointly with other workers, whether to bring it in or not. On several occasions, seamen refused to bring tankers to the jetty if they were covered by the strike. If any undesirable ships got through, shore workers would refuse to couple the pipelines, while seamen threatened that, if replacement workers did the coupling, they would not take the tankers away. At the nearby Esso refinery, Seamen's Union members allowed a small tanker to berth in the interests of essential services; when the company attempted to move it to service another tanker, workers refused to interrupt their job. Forty members of 10 different unions continued thereafter to meet regularly and even considered the formation of a Westernport T&LC.

As late as 1978, 1,600 workers at the Williamstown Naval Dockyard (Melbourne) sacked the dockyard management after a safety dispute and worked for eight days without supervision, defying the interventions of supervisors and management representatives. They elected their own supervisors and determined the allocation of certain work. When it became difficult to find work that they could do, the health and safety committee simply drew up a list of work needed to improve dockyard safety, and workers undertook those tasks. One worker interviewed by *Link* said that the work-in was not only over the safety issue, but also over the question of who has the right to determine work procedures – 'the workers through their trade union or the Navy Brass.'[92]

CHAPTER 6
Worker and Union Ownership

Worker cooperatives, where independent enterprises are owned and controlled by their workers, appeared in Australia in the 19th century, reaching the peak of their popularity in the 1860s. At the same time, consumer cooperatives (stores owned by community members or consumers themselves) were more common. These were inspired significantly by the British Rochdale cooperative, a worker-owned store established in 1844 to protect low-income industrial workers from price gouging. The militancy of workers in this period, inspired by early socialist ideas, was an important factor in the initial growth in cooperatives. Cooperatives have remained a feature of economic life in Australia, although they declined after the 1860s. Agricultural cooperatives, based on countercultural ideas, were set up in the late 1960s. They were a related, although different, phenomenon, concerned more with escaping capitalism than reforming it. One sympathetic historian of the back-to-the-land cooperative movement in the 1960s writes:

> the social ferment of the 1960s has given prominence to the idea of cultural, as opposed to political, radicalism ... for cultural radicals it is the *self-directed living of life* (rather than any contest for power) that is the primary aim.[93]

Rather than just dropping out of the system, trade unionists and union cooperatives had often sought to change it.

NYMBOIDA

On a number of occasions, rank-and-file workers not only seized control of their enterprises; they also seized ownership. This constituted the most radical challenge by far to the power of capital and the state during the 1970s. These acts of direct appropriation, while isolated, represented a radical departure from ordinary trade unionism, providing a bridge between capitalist ownership and direct ownership by workers. Direct appropriation evolved out of work-ins and sit-ins. The work-ins especially raised questions about the need for capitalist ownership. Such questions were often in the background during major work-ins. At the 1972 South Clifton work-in, for example, the local Miners' Federation lodge demanded union ownership of the mine, and some workers even raised ideas of socialism. One miner said of his experience of self-management: 'It gives you a bit of an idea of how it would be to work under socialism, without bosses.'[94]

For some unionists, worker-ownership was perceived as a necessary extension of control. Three years after the South Clifton work-in, workers at Nymboida Collieries, a small coal mine based in the isolated NSW town of Grafton, took a radical new step. In February 1975, the company announced the closure of the mine and the dismissal of all workers, citing slowing profitability. It seemed unlikely that the workforce would receive severance pay. A meeting held in the local pub resolved to continue work the following Monday. Immediate support came from the union movement and the broader public. The Newcastle Trades Hall Council declared that the action was an example to other unionists facing sackings, and officials of the Miners' Federation actively endorsed the action. Following failed negotiations, the union argued that, because the company was absent from meetings, it 'has abdicated from any authority which it might have claimed at Nymboida and has vacated its ownership by default.' The union then demanded that the company surrender its leases and that the State take over ownership – but without success.

Workers next staged a new work-in. They arrived to find a number of obstructions: fuses pulled from switch boxes, switches padlocked and other equipment sabotaged. Nonetheless, they got the mine going. A

CHAPTER 6: WORKER AND UNION OWNERSHIP

Workers at Nymboida mine work-in 1975.
Photo courtesy CFMEU Mining and Energy.

truck driver employed by a local contractor pitched in to help with pit-top jobs. A retired 79-year old miner helped by felling timber for props. Workers lost no pay, because wages were paid by the union. On 3 March, the company relinquished ownership of the mine, handing over all leases and equipment to the Miners' Federation, which also took over all liabilities. The following year, the union set up a new company which it owned and operated. The mine was to be 'controlled by the membership of Nymboida, in conjunction with this Central Council.' The management committee consisted of the leadership of the local Miners' Federation lodge representing members at Nymboida.[95]

The Nymboida experiment galvanised workers across industry. Pat Huxley, former Nymboida miners' lodge president, expressed some of the sentiment:

CHAPTER 6: WORKER AND UNION OWNERSHIP

Workers at Nymboida mine work-in 1975.
Photo courtesy CFMEU Mining and Energy.

> Take a few pictures of us working with a happy look on our faces; then send the pictures to the old Nymboida company and ask them if they've got any other mines which the Miners' Federation can take over.

Vic West, lodge president for much of the time of the Federation ownership, said:

> There is a big difference here between how it is now and how it used to be under the Nymboida company. There isn't a boss breathing down your neck. There is more contentment. That doesn't mean to say we're not working. We're probably working a bit harder still than we had to before, but there's a difference.

By the time the seam was exhausted and the mine closed in 1979, workers had had four years to consider their next move, and the Miners' Federation assisted many into new employment.[96]

WHYALLA GLOVE COOPERATIVE

In early 1973, women employed at the James North Glove factory in Whyalla in SA staged a sit-in at their factory after being made redundant. When one was physically assaulted by the manager, members of the Painters & Dockers Union joined the sit-in to provide security. Eventually, the owner abandoned the factory, allowing the employees to convert it to a workers' cooperative. Verity Burgmann describes it:

> productivity was improved by co-operative work practices. On the shop floor, there existed collective authority and a commitment to collective production. If an individual worker was not pulling their weight, instead of being reprimanded by an authoritarian manager, the whole group would talk to her and, according to one interviewee, 'give encouragement rather than abuse or threats'.

In a turn of events that highlights some of the social contradictions of the period, many of the women's husbands were not very supportive of the new cooperative venture. According to the women, their husbands believed that extra responsibility at the factory disrupted the 'family routine.' The women elected a male foreman, Jim Gettings, on the grounds that he had the necessary skills to repair and maintain the machines. While he remained accountable to the workers via a committee of management, comprised of three women, he managed to get away with being paid six times what the women were paid.

Eventually, the workers voted in September to return the plant to private ownership, on condition that they retained their jobs. In selling the plant to Spencer Gulf Clothing, they conceded even the right to self-management. One woman at the plant resigned and 'refused to work ever again', having been 'spoilt' by her experience with self-management:

> I don't want a bridge between my wages and the product. The company is the middle-man and you can't see any profit unless it is a co-operative—and therefore, for me, there is no incentive to work for the SGC or any other company.

Jim Gettings, the foreman during and after the cooperative period, recalls that, after private ownership was re-established, the workers 'didn't care' about issues of discipline or work ethic: 'They played up,' he recalls, 'always going to the toilet, arguing, complaining' – even refusing to call him 'Mr. Gettings', as he demanded. This sort of attitude from the foreman must have made the period of self-management more difficult.[97]

NATIONALISATION

In this context of challenges to corporate ownership of industry and resources, there were also calls from unionists for nationalisation of industry. These sometimes converged with demands for workers' self-management. Like most other expressions of workers' control, these demands often arose during disputes, and overwhelmingly in responses to layoffs.

The demand was often raised by shop committees during disputes in manufacturing. In August 1973, workers at the privately owned Commonwealth Aircraft Corporation held mass meetings of several thousand to support the demand for nationalisation of the industry. A rank-and-file coordinating committee was established among workers from all plants, including representatives from both the blue and white-collar areas, for the purpose of discussing nationalisation. Unionists from the publicly owned Government Aircraft Factories at Fisherman's Bend (Melbourne), a state-owned enterprise, attended the meetings and gave support. This was their response to layoffs resulting from the downturn and the gradual cessation of military activities in Vietnam, but the call merged with hostility to private profiteering at public expense.

Similar currents ran beneath the surface of other disputes. Two prominent disputes in Brisbane reflect the nationalisation demand. During the 1972 Pillar Naco occupation, a mass meeting of the 700 workers demanded the reinstatement of retrenched workers and, if this could not be guaranteed, that the government should take the factory over. In response to the announcement that the Evans Deakin shipyards in Brisbane would be closed in early 1973, a mass meeting of 800 workers called on the Federal government to take over the shipyards and run them as a government enterprise with worker involvement in management. The influence of Yugoslavia was mentioned earlier; in this period, some workers and unions perceived it to be a viable system of self-management supported by the state. Nonetheless, demands for nationalisation came overwhelmingly from rank-and-file unionists confronted by the exigencies of joblessness and hardship. While the Evans Deakin campaign did not result in nationalisation, the shipyards remained open until 1976.

The issue of nationalisation had an important bearing on workers' control. Given the characterising features of the tendency – direct action, self-organisation and self-management – demands for nationalisation by the state might seem an odd fit. But it is clear why militant unionists might reject state intervention, where its aim was to curtail their activities, yet demand state intervention when it seemed to offer solutions, such as equal pay legislation or government regulation of prices and other commercial activities. Perhaps some workers hoped, when the period of prolonged growth began slowing towards yet another bust cycle at the end of the 1960s, that nationalisation would bring stability to their employment. Some expressed a belief that state-controlled industry would be better coordinated and managed in the interests of workers and the public rather than for private profit. Some unions, like the AEU, contained demands for nationalisation in their constitutions.

WWF members took national strike action in August 1965 for a broad log of claims that included nationalisation of the industry in the interests of planning and stability. Nationalisation had been ALP policy, supported firmly by the left wing of the party. Bill Hartley, State Secretary of the Victorian ALP between 1965 and 1970, advocated for extensive nationalisation of major private enterprises. Gough Whitlam had also campaigned on the issue but retreated from it upon winning office. Many left wing unionists felt strongly about this betrayal. During a strike in 1974 at Wattie Pict, the giant food processing plant in Melbourne, an AMWU shop steward, Greg Pettiona, bitterly denounced the ALP: 'when Labor first came to power, everyone was talking about nationalisation,' but they had since 'forgotten who they represent' and 'that they are the political wing of the trade union movement.'[98] Upon winning office, the ALP actually allowed increased use of private contractors in the public sector, a step short of privatisation. Militant opposition from unions was forthcoming. During the 1973 work-in at the Newcastle docks, workers bitterly condemned the Public Works Department for retrenching public employees while promoting private contracting. Several days before the work-in, a large group of unionists demonstrated at the opening of a bridge over the Williams River. The State Minister was heckled with chants of 'We Want Work' and 'How's the Minister for Private Enterprise?'

Retrenchments in Public Works were linked directly to the use of private contractors. Keith Wilson, secretary of the Newcastle Trades Hall Council, drove the point home:

> The department has the equipment, the know-how and the work-force to do these jobs. It is ironic that PWD employees were called in to complete this bridge after the original contractors went broke.[99]

Prime Minister Whitlam's administration, lauded by some for its progressive stance on social and economic affairs, actually helped to solidify the trend towards privatisation of public industries.

CREDIT UNIONS AND COOPERATIVE STORES

Worker and union ownership took different forms. Some were fairly conventional actions by unions for the purposes of providing services to members; others were more radical. Credit unions took off in the 1960s as a result of larger proportions of aggregate wealth owned by working people. The first credit union in NSW was established in the early 1940s. By 1972, there were 400 credit unions, with 275,000 members and $85 million in assets.

The FIA was particularly active in the area of credit unions for workers. It set up the Ironworkers' Credit Cooperative in 1972 to provide cheap credit to members. It also actively promoted credit union formation, because credit cooperatives could undercut commercial interest rates on loans and finance. The FIA was a more conservative union, with a reactionary, anti-communist leadership. Arguably, its credit schemes were a purely commercial arrangement which had little to do with workers' control from below. In some ways, this was a precursor to today's unions offering movie tickets and store discounts. Nevertheless, the credit unions of the FIA benefited its membership and, for better or worse, represented union ownership of financial services, absent a profit motive. The FIA opposed a proposal by the ACTU to establish a National Union Hire Purchase scheme, advocating instead a national credit union for union members, not wanting to encourage more workers to accept hire purchase schemes. Laurie Short advocated for the purchase of goods through credit union loans, at much more favourable interest rates than hire purchase.

The FIA moved on to establishing building societies. The Sydney-based Cooperative Building Society was the first, in 1974, owned by its members through a buy-in scheme. This institution provided low-cost home loans to members, capitalised through start-up finance of $400,000 from the Federal government. Within a year, it had approved 22 loans for building and home purchases for Sydney FIA members alone.

Cooperative stores were another entity that flourished in this period. The Illawarra Cooperative Store in Wollongong, established in 1970, was owned and operated entirely by its members. By mid-1972, it had tripled in size. The ACTU bought out the Bourke's store in Melbourne, selling a wide range of consumer goods at prices favourable to wage earners. Again, the project did result in some gains for the working class. In late 1970, a number of large manufacturers and wholesalers refused to supply Bourke's, on the grounds that it refused to recognise retail price maintenance (an automatic mark-up). Supported by its affiliate unions, the ACTU selected the Dunlop corporation for retribution in March 1971, black banning all work for the company if it did not supply to Bourke's. Within 24 hours, Dunlop gave in and agreed to supply Bourke's, with no price restrictions. Other manufacturers followed suit, and the Federal government legislated against retail price maintenance. Prime Minister McMahon, not sympathetic to unions, was forced to concede that the ACTU 'got a little in front' of the government in its action on prices.

On the whole, the left wing unions were not supportive of unions entering into enterprise ventures like Bourke's. The AMWU argued that the Bourke's project had not achieved serious price reductions and offered 'no permanent solution to the many economic and social problems facing workers and their families.' It criticised the ACTU for proposing partnerships with private enterprise in construction and tourism, asserting: 'The job of the trade union movement should be to beat the system of private profit, not to join it.'[100] The major issue seemed to be that the ACTU was entering into support for for-profit enterprise arrangements, quite different even from the FIA schemes. Still, left wing unions themselves were not averse to property ownership in support of admirable aims. After the Queensland government refused the Moa Island Indigenous community in Torres Strait permission for a bakery in 1968, the WWF set one up for them by levying its membership. The union also opened a cottage in Dubbo (NSW) to Aboriginal people visiting the Dubbo Base Hospital and who were denied accommodation in the town.

OTHER ACTIONS

At certain times, unionists acted to secure employment for themselves by negotiating contracts for their employers or trying to affect government policy. While this raises the issue of support for private enterprise, what left wing critics called class collaboration, it nevertheless demonstrated high levels of self-activity and self-organisation among rank-and-file trade unionists.

In early 1972, at the historic mining community of Broken Hill, the Broken Hill South company announced that it would close its mine there and retrench 650 workers, leaving up to 20 percent of the workforce unemployed. The workers, supported by the community and the local union, the Workers' Industrial Union (WIU), held a mass meeting on 7 May to demand nationalisation of the mine. Evan Phillips, on behalf of the Miners' Federation, demanded that Broken Hill's leases be forfeited and the mine be taken over by the union itself, as would happen at Nymboida a few years later. When approaches to the government proved futile, the WIU and Miners' Federation approached a small Adelaide-based company, Minerals Mining and Metallurgy (MMM); in October, the mine reopened under their ownership. While the role of a union in securing a new capitalist for a coal mine is questionable, the workers claimed it as a tremendous victory because their jobs were retained and aspects of workplace democracy were instituted. A rank-and-file committee had decision-making powers within the mine; the WIU president, Arthur Treglown, became a member of the MMM board; and a workers' equity scheme returned a large proportion of the company's profits to the workers. However, in May 1976, MMM itself closed the mine in the context of recession and spiralling government charges, giving workers three months' notice and securing work elsewhere for all who would take it.

In this vein, there are several examples in which workers acted to gain work for themselves by securing contracts for their employers. This was particularly common in state-owned manufacturing and engineering. After the Whitlam government ended Australian military involvement in Vietnam, mass meetings at Maribyrnong Explosive, Gordon Street Ammunition and Government Aircraft Factory in Victoria demanded

CHAPTER 6: WORKER AND UNION OWNERSHIP 111

alternative work programs as defence contracts declined. Alongside private sector war industries employees who were demanding nationalisation, a mass meeting of Commonwealth defence workers resolved in September 1973 that:

> while welcoming the re-allocation of Military expenditure into areas of Education, Health and Social Welfare ... Government establishments should be maintained at full employment capacity and should not have to base their work future on the ebb and flow of the Military requirements of this country.'[101]

The meeting resolved that workers would refuse to accept dismissals and that shop stewards would actively investigate alternative work. When the Federal government established an Alternative Work Committee in 1974, it was welcomed, although a mass meeting of defence workers reiterated demands for rank and file representation on the Committee and warned that they would not accept dismissals. They did not wait for an invitation, resolving that each establishment form rank-and-file committees to gather information on alternative work.

In another example, Clyde Master workers, employed on government contracts to build trains, became concerned in 1978 when only three months' worth of contracts remained at the workshop. Believing that the company management had done little to ensure further work, the shop committee met with the shadow Minister of Transport and secured an extension of the contract for a further 54 cars. *Link* reported:

> due to their own initiative workers at Clydemaster have successfully fought off the threat of heavy retrenchments and have again shown their bosses something about how their job should be done.[102]

After the Harco work-in, there was ongoing discussion about ideas for extending workers' control over management, tendering for work in the name of the company, with enquiries to be made to the boilermakers' delegate, and even opening a bank account in the name of the Harco workers. While these were merely proposals, they reflect a high level of workers' initiative and self-activity.

At the Pilkington Glass factory, ETU member Ken Purdham and others on the shop committee made similar approaches to the Federal Treasurer after the removal of tariffs on glass imports resulted in a sales dip and the retrenchment of 66 workers in 1975. In response, the Federal government restored the tariffs, and all retrenched workers were reinstated. Such was the strength and independence of the shop committee organisation, that it was able to influence government policy.

CHAPTER 7
Radical Unions Beyond the Workplace

OPPOSITION TO ANTI-STRIKE LAWS

Rank-and-file unionists challenging the authority of the boss at the enterprise level were also eager to challenge the rights and prerogatives of governments and employers in the social and political domains. Many participants, particularly the CPA, saw political strikes, bans and similar actions as a kind of workers' control beyond the workplace. They argued that these actions sprang from the same fundamental urge as work-ins and radical trade unionism, reflecting a surge in democratic worker and community power. No longer were ordinary people content just to sit back and let decisions about their lives simply be made for them by commercial and political elites. Rank-and-file union members were very active in trade union political interventions from the later 1960s, although their effectiveness was often dependent on alliances with community organisations and the broader public. The role of union officials was variable. Sometimes, their cooperation was necessary. Sometimes, shop committees and ordinary workers acted with relative autonomy. Occasionally, rank-and-file initiatives were frustrated by union officials, particularly those within the ACTU.

By far the most successful intervention of workers into political affairs was the near total neutralisation of anti-strike laws throughout the entire 1970s. After the successful defeat of the penal powers in 1969, the threat of legal sanction for industrial action was removed in all but the most radical cases, such as work-ins and occupations. A major 1971 strike at Commonwealth Engineering (Comeng) in Sydney shows the militancy of ordinary workers in opposing anti-strike powers.

At Comeng, the use of penal provisions under the Arbitration Act and stand-down clauses within the Metal Trades Award quickly became the main issue in a dispute which started over wages. To coincide with a meeting between ACTU officials and Comeng over the strike, another meeting of over 700 shop stewards from all metal unions resolved to refuse payment of all fines, regardless of the 'official' decision by union leaders and other officials. In the end, the AEU, Blacksmiths & Boilermakers' Society and Sheet Metal Workers' Union refused to pay the ensuing fines, as did the Moulders' Union for a separate strike in 1971. With the threat of a repeat of 1969, the fines were again paid by another anonymous donor.

In the same year, the introduction of new penal powers by the South Australian Labor government, with support from the T&LC, provoked rank-and-file anger. Jim Moss pointed out some of the contradictions within the union movement:

> union delegates to the T&LC who voted for the S.A. Government's legislation did so knowing full well that the trade union movement as a whole had already decided to the contrary ... There are many instances where the workers are forced to exert wasteful time and energy in order to express their will in their own trade unions [against] trade union bureaucrats who see office as a means to further their own careers in the trade union movement or Labor Party.

Only a few weeks prior to the introduction of the legislation, the State Secretary of the AWU, Jim Dunford, had refused to pay fines arising from the Kangaroo Island dispute over union hire. Facing the threat of a mass strike, the Government itself paid the fines. Moss described a feeling among unionists that it had done this to 'head off a full-scale confrontation between the unions and the employers.'[103]

The opposition of rank-and-file unionists to anti-strike laws was demonstrated again and again throughout the period. Early in 1971, members of the Victorian Teachers' Union took a series of strike actions over a log of claims. Some 40 Victorian secondary schools held strikes throughout March and April, demanding reduced class sizes, the removal of unqualified teachers from schools and reductions in 'contact time.'

In response, the Bolte government proposed the imposition of harsh penalties for the strikers, undoubtedly hoping to test out the penalties for use elsewhere among state sector employees. One sanction was that teachers would lose a year of long service leave credits for every day on which they defied the anti-strike order. In direct response to the government's order, teachers planned mass strike action, with 8,000 teachers attending strike meetings across Victoria. The government relented.

One of the Coalition government's more blustering policies came in 1977 in the form of an Industrial Relations Bureau (IRB), a sort of industrial relations police force with expanded powers to arrest and charge unionists. Announcement of the IRB was met with immediate strikes and stoppages. Eight thousand workers and shop stewards, including 1500 dockyard workers, struck to attend mass meetings in Victoria. Such was the display of resistance that the IRB was rendered, in the words of *Link*, 'a paper tiger.' As late as June 1979, ten officials of the AMWSU were charged under the *Western Australian Police Act* for holding a public meeting without permission. Amidst an immediate state-wide threat of export bans, transport blockades and 'widespread industrial dislocation' by members of the AMWSU and other unions, another anonymous donor paid all outstanding fines.

Union members saw their actions in defying anti-strike laws as a moral imperative. It was their fundamental right to take strike action on their own terms and at their own discretion, and they would oppose any attempt by the state to impede them. This comes back to some fundamental points about democracy – many unionists saw their unions as the organisations that represented them when it came to industrial and economic affairs. Without unions, they would be left at the mercy of politicians and policymakers who had no experience or understanding of their day-to-day lives. Many also saw shop and site committees as being

Moratorium posters "Stop work to stop the war".

in the position to exercise this power. A mass meeting of Victorian AMWU delegates in 1973 affirmed their ongoing opposition to anti-strike laws, declaring that they were:

> firmly opposed to any agreement or consent award which precludes metal workers from exercising their inherent right to struggle on an individual shop or group basis for improvements in wages rates or working conditions.

For many union workers, it was their *inherent right* to take collective action over their working conditions, and so it was their duty to defy any system of laws that attempted to curtail it.

Governments responded in different ways to the rejection of anti-strike laws by unions. It is interesting to speculate about the identity of the anonymous benefactors who consistently paid off union fines when it came down to a confrontation. It was rumoured that the fines were paid by the Australian Security Intelligence Organisation, although it may also have been the initiative of the large employers' associations who sought to avoid the catastrophe of losing a major battle against the unions. Although it seems counterintuitive, the fines were paid not to do the unions any sort of favour, but to prevent them from demonstrating the full extent of their ability to ignore the law. Payment of the fines allowed governments and employers to avoid a series of humiliating defeats and – perhaps even more significantly – prevented unionists from realising just how powerful their organisations had become.

As a direct result of union pressure, the ALP was forced to remove strike penalties from its policy program in 1971. Despite ongoing pressure from employer groups, this remained the policy throughout the brief term of the Whitlam government. After 1975, the Liberal–Country Party Coalition, led by Malcolm Fraser, sought to shore up the legislative power necessary to bring the union movement to heel. Fraser's legal reforms represented not so much a return to the penal provisions of the 1950s and 1960s as a considerable extension of them, but the strength of the union movement meant that he was unable to use them. One industrial relations scholar coolly observed that industrial penal powers for the purposes of policing unions were:

> subject to the same fundamental limitation as all sanctioning devices in the industrial-relations context— they can work only so long as those to whom the sanctions are directed are prepared to allow them to work.

In other words, if a large enough proportion of the population took strike action (and had sufficient power to hold the strike), there was little that a relative handful of politicians and police could do about it. Industrial sociologist Alex Carey reached a similar conclusion, observing that 'Fraser obtained all the anti-union legislation he needed', but:

> could not use it because his specially conducted opinion polls continued to tell him that such action would not have enough public support to be viable.

It was not until the 1980s that the law was used to smash the unions.[104]

UNION ACTION AGAINST WAR AND MILITARISM

Trade unionists provided the most powerful and consistent opposition to the Vietnam War. One reason for this was that CPA-aligned union leaders had a political interest in preventing Australian aggression against Communist North Vietnam. The strategic positioning of these unions on the docks and in the munitions industries also enabled significant impact. However, union interventions to stop the war were also motivated significantly by humanitarian concerns for the victims of the war throughout South East Asia, whose suffering was broadcast live across Australian television screens for the first time.

As early as June 1962, Melbourne watersiders refused to load barbed wire bound for Vietnam and condemned the Australian Government for 'interference in the affairs of another country.' This action showed a striking degree of international awareness among watersiders. Australia had only deployed a few dozen military advisers to Vietnam in 1962 – combat troops would not be deployed there until 1965. It was also years before the mass student protests and other actions that are typically associated with the anti-war movement. The major Vietnamese transport union responded from Hanoi with words of thanks, saying that the wire would have been used 'to encircle concentration camps for gaoling South Vietnamese workers and people.' By this stage, the Australian-backed South Vietnamese dictatorship had indeed jailed more political prisoners than every other government on earth combined.[105]

The ACTU, however, declared in 1966 that, while the war against Vietnam would be condemned, Australian unions would not interfere with the carriage of goods to Vietnam. The Seamen's Union defied the ban immediately. Seamen refused to load barbed wire on board the *Boonaroo*. The militant WWF was facing deregistration at that time if its record of industrial unrest continued, so the union leadership decided not to risk a national stoppage when Australian combat troops were first deployed to Vietnam in 1965. But rank-and-file WWF members could not be brought into line. In September 1967, in the longest running union ban on war-related work, more than 2,500 watersiders refused to work on the Navy supply vessel *Jeparit*, which served as the major

Workers support anti-Vietnam war protest 1967.
Unknown photographer.

supplier to Australian forces in Vietnam. Members of the Seamen's Union also refused.

Watersiders again refused to load the vessel in 1969. Their delegate, Harry Black, was suspended for a month, provoking stoppages of 4,000 Sydney WWF members. In April 1971, 50 wharfies at Port Kembla stopped work on a ship bound for Saigon upon learning that it was loaded with steel. After deciding to accept the companies' claim that it was for housing, they resumed work.

The idea of rank-and-file unionists stopping work and holding a meeting to discuss the social purposes and implications of their work, debating whether or not to continue, negotiating with employers and managers on their own terms and then voting, paints a picture of real workplace democracy. Indeed, the political life of the WWF was dependent on high levels of self-organisation by ordinary workers.

Despite the mass anti-war movement, large numbers of Australians supported the war, and these divisions were represented within unions.

Unions and committees thus served as organisations for education and discussion of the war, not simply as a means to make political incursions. Large-scale anti-war demonstrations were held in 1969. Unionists involved in anti-war activities campaigned around the slogan: 'Stop Work to Stop the War.' Brian Dunnett, a railway worker and a representative of the rank-and-file Trade Union Moratorium committee, discussed the conflicted nature of the anti-war moratoriums among unionists. He noted that, in the metal trades which led the campaign, most sites that he visited voted by a narrow majority against strike action. Dunnett wrote:

> A similar story can be told in most industries, including my own... The main point to come out of the metal trades Moratorium organiser's speech was that with rank-and-file organisation plus official union assistance, an atmosphere of debating the issues can be created and result in workers taking a more informed stand, for or against.[106]

Tens of thousands of workers did join in 'Stop Work to Stop the War' campaigns through 1970–1971. Frank Cherry remembers that he and other officials would regularly visit Victorian metal factories to discuss the war with members before voting to stop work, and that rank-and-file education was vital to the campaign. He contrasts the activity of the AEU with that of the conservative Amalgamated Society of Engineers (ASE) who:

> weren't politicising their members. They didn't think it was appropriate to be involved with the members politically, whereas the AEU organisers deliberately went out and were political.

Anti-war unionists also made efforts to engage the public in debates over the war, leading to a wider discussion of the role of unions. When the Melbourne City Council passed a by-law banning the handing out of anti-war leaflets in city streets at the end of 1968, the Victorian rebel unions banned all work on Courage beer and Paterson's furniture stores; one council bureaucrat was executive director of both companies. Strikes against the war by the WWF sparked the ire of *The Australian*. After a bitter attack on the union in an editorial, a reader wrote in *Tribune*:

> as far as *The Australian* is concerned it is fine to make humanitarian noises about war, and even, in certain circumstances, fine for unions to increase the purchasing-power of their members, but when unionists, without any thought of economic gain, seek to disrupt the making of profits for the purpose of gaining a political objective, then all Hell has broken loose among the capitalists, whether of Left or Right.[107]

These controversies raise important questions over the function of unions: should they serve as more than just organisations for collective bargaining over wages and conditions? Left wing trade unions argued that unions should also be political and social organisations within which working people could discuss issues of greater public significance. Others argued that unions should be confined to everyday industrial affairs; politics was for the politicians.

Anti-war activism was not confined to the waterfront unions. When the US-backed South Vietnamese dictator Nguyen Cao Ky made an official visit to Australia in 1967, rank-and-file metal unionists refused to service his plane, resulting in the use of army labour.

The issue of conscription was a major source of conflict. Many young workers in unions actively supported each other in resistance to the draft. *Link* was published by John Cleary and other young CPA members from a Melbourne safe-house for draft resisters. In April 1969, the Miners' Federation Central Council carried a motion resolving that their union would act in defence of its members if they resisted the draft and were arrested. The Central Council of Railway Shop Committees did the same and also refused to make union records available to the police.

Opposition to the war also had an effect on the relationship between union members and officials. As with the penal power issue, anti-war

union leaders found that their freedom from police harassment and arrest depended on the rank-and-file members of their unions. In September 1969, after Laurie Carmichael was arrested at an anti-conscription protest in Melbourne, 500 workers at the Williamstown Naval Dockyard stopped work, and Victorian unions threatened strike action, securing Carmichael's release. This mutual support between members and officials existed also among the Blacksmiths & Boilermakers, whose members threatened nationwide stoppages if their officials were jailed for signing a statement encouraging men to defy the *National Service Act*. Other union bodies were more conservative. In January 1973, the BWIU proposed to the NSW Labour Council that all affiliated unions implement

Moratorium badges belonging to Ken Mansell including 'Stop work to stop the war'. Photo courtesy Ken Mansell.

industrial sanctions if US bombing of South East Asia resumed, and that, if the US did not sign a peace agreement by the end of the month, that US goods and services be boycotted in Australia. The Labour Council was happy enough to put out a statement condemning US aggression in Vietnam but, in a familiar pattern by this stage, recommended that any industrial action over international matters be left to the ACTU.

Alongside opposition to the war, unionists took a range of actions in opposition to other kinds of militarism and state violence. Proposals to build the American Omega satellite base provoked threats of union bans in August 1973. Leaders of FEDFA argued that 'unionists have a responsibility to see that their labour is not devoted to anti-social ends' and declared:

> we will recommend to our members that they refuse to supply their labour for the prefabrication of materials, or for the actual construction, of an Omega installation in this country.

As well as the broader implications of their actions, unionists were also concerned about their own *personal* responsibility for the social costs of their work. After all, workers are responsible for building weapons and other tools of state violence, so it makes sense that they might have a stake in decisions around the work. Other work bans came from the rank and file. Tony Robins, an ETU steward at the Cerberus Naval Dockyard, recalls bitter conflicts between Navy personnel and civilian maintenance workers, stirred up by the Vietnam War. When naval police targeted maintenance workers with speed cameras, they black banned maintenance work on the officers' toilets, quickly producing a resolution.[108]

As early as 1963, the WWF had issued a statement condemning French nuclear testing in the Pacific. In 1964 it ran a leaflet campaign against tests, although it was not until 1972 that the WWF began to impose bans on French ships and aircrafts. When it was rumoured that the HMAS *Supply* would move into the Pacific alongside the HMNZS *Canterbury* to oppose French nuclear testing, in an unusual twist, workers at Garden Island in Sydney lifted all bans and limitations on overtime in order to have the ship ready as quickly as possible. In response, dockyard management and the Navy tried to delay the process, so that the ship would not reach the test zone in time. After efforts to confirm the rumour failed, members of the Painters and Dockers Union defied management and allowed the *Supply* to enter the yards. When the bosses cut their work teams from three to two, the workers walked off, held a mass meeting at the front gate and staged a sit-in. They telegrammed the government offering to carry out the refit of the ship without oversight from the Navy and, incredibly, more than 100 dock workers volunteered to crew the ship on its voyage. It is unclear how the dispute was resolved, although the *Supply* did sail from Sydney to Mururoa Atoll in June 1973 to protest French nuclear testing.

STRUGGLES FOR REPRESENTATION AND EQUALITY

The NSWBLF was an international pioneer in the area of social strikes. Of the more than $3 billion (at 1970s prices) worth of development obstructed by so-called green bans across NSW, most was for social and community, rather than environmental, issues. One of the most high-profile bans occurred in November 1971, in defence of working-class housing at The Rocks on the western side of Sydney Cove. The area was almost entirely under public ownership, with the Maritime Services Board acting as landlord to the various sailors, wharfies and pensioners, as well as cleaners and shop assistants, inhabiting it. The Sydney Cove Redevelopment Authority, established in January 1970, announced its intention to convert the area into high-rise office blocks. The union banned the project in 1971. A four-year stand-off followed, during which actions included the 'Battle for The Rocks' in 1973, a day when one site was occupied by locals and two union officials, Jack Mundey and Joe Owens. Both Mundey and Owens were arrested. Eventually, the union and its supporters won a new development plan in 1975.

Similar action by the NSWBLF saved the low-income housing settlement at Woolloomooloo. The government wanted to convert the working-class area to office and hotel blocks, separated by the projected Eastern Expressway. In February 1973, a green ban halted the demolition of homes. A more moderate scheme was also rejected by residents and union members (many of whom lived in Woolloomooloo), and the ban was only lifted in 1975 after the announcement of an extensive program of community involvement. The NSW Institute for Urban Development acknowledged the NSWBLF for demonstrating the need for community participation in redevelopment projects.

Property developer Frank Theeman's plan to evict 300 people and convert historic houses in Victoria Street, Kings Cross, into high-rise buildings was also stopped in its tracks by the imposition of a green ban in 1973, despite Theeman's use of hired criminals to vandalise the properties and render them unlivable. There were also bans in defence of working-class neighbourhoods through much of Sydney, including Surry

Hills and Newtown, and also Northgate and in Newcastle's East End.

The NSWBLF imposed the world's first pink bans. In June 1973, a global precedent was set when the union placed a pink ban on all new construction at Macquarie University (Sydney) after a student, Jeremy Fisher, was expelled for involvement in gay liberation activities. Fisher, treasurer of the campus Gay Liberation Group, was recovering from an attempted suicide when the Master of his campus college, Alan Cole, discovered gay liberation materials in his room and expelled him. The student council turned to the NSWBLF, who responded immediately with a work ban. Fisher chose not to return to Macquarie – he went on to become a prolific writer and Director of the Australian Society of Authors. The NSWBLF maintained its commitment to freedom of sexuality at Macquarie later in 1973. When Penny Short, studying to become a teacher, was stripped of her scholarship because of her sexuality, the union again imposed a pink ban. Joe Owens said:

> NSW Builders Labourers Federation condemns the Education Department for discrimination against Penny Short. If her scholarship is not returned, bans will be placed on maintenance work by builders' labourers on Education Department buildings and other Government offices.[109]

The Teachers' Federation offered some support, helping to organise a march and a public meeting. It is not clear how the campaign ended, although Short's scholarship was not returned to her.

Racism was pervasive in the 1970s, and the union movement was often at the forefront of struggles to oppose it. Unions joined student and community groups in 1966 in donating to the struggle of Gurindji workers in the Northern Territory, after they and community members walked off the Wave Hill station in protest against unpaid wages and decades of mistreatment by the white pastoralists who owned the station. The AEU, Blacksmiths & Boilermakers' Society and Sheet Metal Workers Union became the first unions to impose bans on 'negotiation with any companies seeking awards or agreements for construction of plants for the purpose of plunder of natural resources on land claimed by Aborigines.' They boycotted the Vesteys Brothers (who owned the station) and Nabalco. Eventually, other unions joined the boycott and called upon the ACTU in 1971 to 'impose a "dual boycott" in the fight against racism' against the national rugby team of apartheid South Africa and two companies, Vesteys and Nabalco, for acquiring Aboriginal land.

The ACTU did urge its affiliates to take 'whatever action is necessary as an act of conscience' to disrupt the South African rugby team in its tour of Australia in 1971, in contrast to its tepid support for anti-war activities. When the repressive Bjelke-Petersen government in Queensland brought in new police powers to manage the South African rugby tour of 1971, unions across the state imposed bans and strikes with the support of the Queensland T&LC. A mass meeting of striking workers at the Brisbane Exhibition Ground declared opposition to the 'state-of-emergency' measures. A special meeting of the NSW Liquor & Allied Industries Union in April 1971 announced a total ban on all labour and supplies going to sports grounds where South African teams appeared. Waterfront unions in Sydney held monthly eight-hour stoppages in the lead up, and the Seamen's Union blacked goods and passengers associated with South African sporting tours. The NSW branch of FEDFA endorsed any direct action taken to sabotage and disrupt the tours, and unionists at hotels and other services were encouraged to withhold labour. Port Kembla wharfies pledged strike action if any protestors were arrested. The NSW Theatrical and Amusement Employees Association instructed their members employed on turnstiles or as ticket sellers not to work at fixtures at which South African teams appeared.

The ACTU stand encouraged other unions, such as the Transport Workers, who banned all services (including the provision of fuel) for any plane transporting South African teams to, or within, Australia. As a result of this and other bans, South African teams and others were flown around the country by the Australian Air Force. In June 1971, the ship Safocean *Amsterdam*, which was to carry sheet steel for South Africa, left Port Kembla 'with 250 tons of Lysaght products still on the wharf' after waterside unionists refused to load it. Maritime unions in Sydney also refused, yet again, to handle cargo from the *Jeparit* as it returned from

Vietnam. They announced instead that their labour 'would be readily available should the government indicate a firm and early date for total withdrawal of Australian forces from Vietnam.'[110]

A particularly high-profile action in 1974 demonstrates the willingness of unions to take action on social issues and shows the power that organised workers possessed at the time. In July, a tour of Australia by Frank Sinatra was derailed by union bans after Sinatra made misogynistic comments about women working in the press. Sinatra, frustrated by aspects of his Australian press coverage, described Australian journalists as 'parasites' and 'bums', and female journalists as worth 'a buck and a half.' The Australian Theatrical and Amusement Employees Association, who controlled the lighting and other technical aspects of Sinatra's tour, announced that they would strike until Sinatra apologised. When the singer refused, his Melbourne show had to be cancelled. Bans were agreed upon by several unions until Sinatra apologised. When the singer threatened to leave the country, the TWU refused to service his aircraft; no member at any airport would carry out work for Frank Sinatra. Such was the effectiveness of the ban that Sinatra could not even find hotel workers to carry his bags. When Sinatra finally offered a half-hearted apology, he was able to leave the country.

MEDIBANK AND PRICE CONTROL

The Fraser government's decision to impose levies on Medibank and increase its exposure to private competition provoked widespread stoppages in the metal trades in 1976, involving 40,000 workers in Wollongong alone. A meeting of 1,500 shop stewards in Victoria proposed weekly stoppages in every state as a move towards generalised national strike action, only for it to be diluted to a single four-hour stoppage by the ACTU. Rank-and-file opposition was expressed as direct action on the shop floor. A rash of strikes in metal shops throughout Victoria attempted to force individual employers to provide health insurance, as a response to the failure of the campaign to defend Medibank from the Fraser government. At Philip Morris, 1,200 workers held an immediate 24-hour stoppage, to demand health insurance, and established a works council representing workers from all unions to organise ongoing action. The demand was quickly won at several shops, including Trayco Metal Fabricators and Alcoa, and by the shop committee at B&D Doors.

Link explained that 'Medibank was destroyed by a government which has the full support of all employer groups'; therefore, health insurance should be extracted from individual employers. An AMWU shop steward at Aeron Ventilation in Melbourne framed the struggle in similar terms:

> It appears to me that it is impossible to separate political and economic affairs ... The Medibank strike brought to the notice of all Australians that the Liberal Government are in the process of destroying a good national health scheme. To remain silent would be doing a disservice to the working class.

Employers' associations were worried about the incursion by unions into the affairs of government. Ian Spicer of the Victorian Employers' Federation warned that 'it would be necessary for a government to seek trade union approval before being able to implement the policies on which they were elected.'

Rank and file dynamism over the issue was frustrated by inertia from the union bureaucracy. John Cleary and other editors of *Link* argued that there was a 'deliberate campaign by certain union officials in the Trades Hall Council and ACTU to sabotage rank and file opposition to Fraser's attack', shown by the decision of the ACTU not to call a national stoppage and by Trades Hall overriding decisions made by meetings of shop stewards and job delegates. These, the editors argued, '*directly* represent tens of thousands of workers from all industries.'[111] In contrast, action at the shop floor was widespread.

Prices became an issue of significant public concern in the early 1970s, particularly after the 1973 oil spike. Unionists in shop committees and mass meetings began discussing action, including strategies to achieve price controls. During the 1973 referendum on the subject, FEDFA officials described a demonstration in Melbourne as 'the most broadly based union group ever brought together in Victoria', in support of the 'granting of full power to the Commonwealth to control prices.' When the referendum failed to deliver, some unionists responded with direct action. A meeting of over 200 shop stewards in Victoria endorsed shopfloor action and set up an ongoing organisation to plan consumer boycotts, rallies and industrial action against employers accused of price gouging. AMWU shop stewards held workplaces meetings and established a sub-committee to give direction to the union leadership on a campaign. One Newcastle AMWU shop steward said that members were 'looking for a situation where, short of nationalisation, only a minimum price enabling just a reasonable profit margin should be permitted.' The CPA commented that actions on prices had a radical nature, arguing that capitalism 'centres on the right of the capitalist owner to hire, fire and set the price of his product' and 'any tampering with these "rights" is at the heart of the class struggle.'[112]

Other campaigns were based around more innovative responses to profiteering. During a wage dispute at Cadbury Schweppes in 1976, *Link* exposed plans by the company to increase advertising to children in order to skirt price controls if the Federal government introduced them. On more than one occasion, the WWF banned meat exports in a campaign to force domestic reductions in the price of meat. A long-lasting ban on meat exports, led by CPA members, was imposed by Sydney watersiders in March 1973. The role of unions themselves in pushing the Whitlam government to act on price controls may also have been significant. As early as 1967, Victorian Railway shop committees arranged their own study of prices and profits among major metal industry employers to present to Government.

SUPPORT FOR FOREIGN WORKERS

The lives of foreign workers in shipping were often improved dramatically through the intervention of Australian watersiders and seamen. In June 1969, the *Tia Juana*, a Panamanian flag of convenience ship staffed with Chinese officers, arrived in Fremantle carrying a cargo of urea (chemical fertiliser). The ship carried 26 workers above the official complement, so the predominantly Filipino labourers had insufficient

CHAPTER 7: RADICAL UNIONS BEYOND THE WORKPLACE 131

toilets and washing facilities and no cabins, sleeping on the bagged urea and in the alleyways and cattle fittings. The ship was rat infested, and the urea smelled like unwashed urinals. The combined maritime unions immediately demanded that workers be provided with stretchers, warm bedding and well-ventilated shelter. Hearing the discussions at 5.30 pm, WWF members unanimously decided that if the conditions were not met by 7.30 pm, all labour would be withdrawn from the ship. The demand was swiftly met.

WWF branches would often personally investigate the wages and conditions of foreign workers aboard ships docking in Australia. A Filipino crew of 23 aboard the Greek ship *Paraskevi Yemelos*, docked in Port Kembla, complained directly to the secretary of the Seamen's Union. He intervened on their behalf, securing severance pay and repatriation by air to Manila.

In July 1970, Australian watersiders may well have saved the life of a Greek–Australian union activist who was visiting relatives in Greece. The Greek dictatorship had a long record of 'disappearing' union activists, and Antonios Vrettos, a waterside worker and member of the North Australia Workers' Union in Darwin, was arrested. On learning this, the WWF immediately banned work on a number of Greek ships in ports across Australia, including Sydney and Port Kembla, and stoppages occurred in Melbourne. WWF representatives met with the Greek consul. One official, Norm Docker, attempted to telephone Vrettos. The union executive also threatened to seek a ban on any services to Greek diplomats or officials. Within a few days, Vrettos was released and returned to Australia. Australian unionists were applauded by pro-democracy groups in Greece, including the Democritus League, who formally thanked the WWF for 'boosting the morale of the Greek people and greatly helping the movement against the fascist junta.'[113]

Maritime unions stopped work on the Norwegian ship *Slembe* in August 1971, over the appalling conditions of Chinese and Papua New Guinean crew. The Vigilance Officer of the WWF, Matt Munro – known for his militancy – insisted that all Australian and foreign workers aboard the ship be present for the meeting. Following a brief strike, the crew of the *Slembe* had their wages doubled and were given blankets, soap, pillows, toilet paper and decent meals. In January 1974, the Melbourne WWF blacked the Spanish ship *Pacifico* in protest against the jailing of trade union leaders in fascist Spain. Workers in Sydney again refused labour for 24 hours, with maritime unions investigating the ship and the conditions of the Spanish crew. At the same time, at least 13 Greek ships were stuck in Australian ports because of a national ban by maritime unions in protest against the right wing Greek government, a ban which was actively supported by Greek shipping companies. A Seamen's Union stopwork meeting in Sydney called on their union to contact international trade union bodies to initiate an international ban. In late May, two ships chartered to carry wheat to Chile were held up in Newcastle for several days by union bans in protest against repression of unionists by the Pinochet regime. Another ship, the *Star Lily*, a Greek ship chartered to the Chilean dictatorship, was hit with a total ban by Australian workers, in a blow to two separate fascist regimes.

GREEN BANS AND BEYOND

The British IWC lauded the green bans in 1973 as 'a new advance and contributing and entirely original experience which deserves serious study in Britain.'[114] The NSWBLF shut down large swathes of destructive and offensive development by profiteering developers throughout the early 1970s. In June 1971, they blocked AV Jennings from converting five hectares of green space at Kelly's Bush into houses by threatening bans on all the company's projects in the state. In November 1971, they similarly threatened all the work sites of Parkes Development, who tried to renege on the creation of a park at one of their developments. In March 1972, when the State government attempted to build a carpark for the Sydney Opera House right next to the Botanic Gardens, damaging vegetation, a ban imposed by the NSWBLF resulted in the inclusion of the union in the planning of the build.

These actions and results demonstrate unusually high levels of democracy achieved by the intervention of trade unions. The action at Kelly's Bush followed months of organising and discussion between community members, union members and officials and the Labour Council. The union to

CHAPTER 7: RADICAL UNIONS BEYOND THE WORKPLACE   133

some extent challenged the rights of private property developers to make decisions arbitrarily and, subsequently, the right of bureaucratic state bodies to plan city development without concern for social and environmental consequences. The CPA-dominated leadership of the NSWBLF supported direct action, but impetus also came from the rank and file. Mark Haskell, an industrial relations scholar, attributes the green ban phenomenon to the political orientation of the NSWBLF leadership but admits that the union was characterised by 'adherence to principles of participatory democracy' and was 'anarchic'. He quotes a contemporary CPA observer who described BLF members as having 'contempt for organisation and leadership' and displaying 'the ultra-democracy of spontaneism.'[115]

In June 1972, bans were imposed on 400 acres of ponds, lawns and wilderness at Centennial Park, where the State government proposed construction of a sports stadium. In August 1973, an attempt by Fowler West Industries to turn six hectares of west Sydney forest into a factory was banned by the NSWBLF in cooperation with a local resident action group. The following month, a similar ban was imposed on development of Riley's Island, after 500 people voted unanimously for it at a public meeting. Early in 1974, residents and a network of community groups in the Port Stephens area of the NSW central coast asked the NSWBLF to ban work on indiscriminate high rises, particularly on foreshores. Environmental bans were imposed on any building at Dunbar Park in Sydney, because of rumours that the local council intended to convert it to a rubbish dump; on the construction of a sewage treatment plant in the Wyong Valley on the NSW Central Coast; on Sydney's second airport at Galston on the outskirts of Sydney's green belt; on sand mining at Ebenezer near Windsor; and on any future building development in the Narrabeen Lagoon area.[116] The union's aim was to limit commercial development in the interests of ordinary people and the environment. The close relationship between the unions and local communities, environmental groups, residents' associations and occasionally government bodies reflects an expression of participatory democracy. The combined actions prevented the virtual free rein developers might otherwise have had.

The broader political and industrial relations landscape was influenced by the NSW actions. In Melbourne, the Victorian branch of the union saved a number of heritage sites, including a hotel and the Queen Victoria markets. In Perth, the Western Australian branch imposed a green ban on demolition of the historic Palace Hotel on St. George's Terrace in January 1974, and on Victoria Hall, another historic building, three months later. Green bans also spread to other unions. In 1972, the South Australian branch of the Plumbers' Union imposed a series of its own green bans on residential development around Adelaide, including stock paddocks in the northern suburbs, several acres of land opposite the Parafield aerodrome, and the Penfold vineyard at Magill. The union's State President in SA, R. J. Giles, had only to look to NSW to tell the press: 'We've got a gun at the head of the big land developers and will pull the trigger if necessary.'[117]

Metal unions imposed a number of their own environmental bans. From 1969, Victorian rebel unions led public opposition to the construction of an ethane pipeline across Port Phillip Bay and strongly advocated a ban on a proposal to discharge effluent into Port Phillip at Carrum. The CPA commented:

> The trade union movement did well to take a hand in the affair, which affects the welfare of their members and the rest of the community. A logical next step for the labour movement would be to develop more far-reaching policies on the quality of life of Australian working people.[118]

Several other organisations opposed the proposal, including the Mordialloc Council. Although Trades Hall Council withdrew its ban in July, the 26 rebel unions maintained the ban. Even when work began on the pipeline in October, unions continued a total work ban on all labour. Fifteen police protected the project around the clock until its completion in December.

In January 1970, the Queensland T&LC banned proposed oil drilling on the Great Barrier Reef. Conservationists had tried for some time to stop drilling on the reef, but the Bjelke-Petersen government had ignored them. By the time the ban was imposed, the drilling company was preparing to move equipment from Texas. The ban forced a government Commission of Enquiry into the nature of the drilling and the dangers it posed. The T&LC also insisted that a representative sit on the Commission. The company conducting test drilling reported: 'It is our opinion that industrial action will prevent the drilling of this offshore well when the rig arrives on site.' *Tribune* commented that the Great Barrier Reef struggle:

> shows the tremendous potential for trade union intervention in broad issues, going far beyond those matters of pay and working conditions to which some would limit trade unionism.[119]

Months later, Queensland unions imposed another green ban, this time to protect the Cooloola Sands area north of Brisbane from sand mining. Queensland Titanium Mines and Cudgen Rutile had began acquiring leases in the area in 1963, provoking a public backlash and the formation of a public anti-mining group, the Cooloola Committee. In 1972, an attempt by the same companies to extend their sand mining operations into Cooloola resulted in a ban by all Queensland unions represented by the T&LC, calling on the State government to declare the area a national park. The attempt of the companies to sue the State government was unsuccessful; in 1975, the unions had a victory with the establishment of the Cooloola National Park.

The NSW AMWU imposed environmental bans along the Hawkesbury River, at Botany Bay and the Chullora Container Depot. Frank Bollins acknowledged broad rank-and-file support for these actions – workers would:

> 'as a matter of conscience, drive the machines, turn on the tap, wield the axe and saw—or as a matter of conscience, refuse to do so, and so prevent the project from proceeding.'[120]

Workers in the Queensland sugar industry established a committee of delegates, 'elected from mills and financed by job collections', which organised for 'environmental control' and reduction of 'pollution and noise' which were 'a disability for the communities.'[121] At the Midlands Railway Workshop in Perth, workers took strike action to support a community campaign against a local abattoir because of its 'nauseating smell.' In early 1973, the campaign caused the abattoir to be taken to court.

In Victoria, the most dramatic dispute over the environmental consequences of commercial development was over construction of the Newport Power Station. The Victorian Trades Hall Council banned work on construction of the station from 1974, on the grounds that it would be a heavy polluter. After a temporary backdown, the Hamer government doubled down on its efforts to successfully build the station. This dispute reveals the beginnings of the decline of workers' control along with the impact of the recession. By 1974, unemployment had begun to erode union militancy, and union officials vacillated. Despite most metal unions maintaining a paper commitment, they let it slip in practice, and the project was eventually completed with union labour. The whole affair caused a rift in the union movement. Some union workers began work on the site; others regularly picketed it. Danny Gardiner, an FIA member, refused to work on it and was flatly dismissed. There was significant conflict on the picket line, including a number of fights. When a close friend of his took a job at the site, Gardiner ended their friendship. Years later, a worker was chased out of the Williamstown dockyards when it was discovered that he had worked on construction of the power station.

Some unionists were actively opposed to the construction of new freeways. Green bans between 1973 and 1974 caused plans by the NSW government to expand freeways across the state to be delayed and, in some cases, entirely abandoned. Two major projects – the North-Western and the Eastern expressways – were abandoned as a result of bans by the NSWBLF, working in cooperation with local communities. After public meetings at the inner-city Sydney suburbs of Pyrmont and Ultimo, which were threatened with destruction by the proposed North-Western Expressway, unions imposed green bans in mid-1973; the project was later abandoned. At the request of affected residents, the NSWBLF stopped construction of the Eastern Freeway in its tracks in 1973. The freeway was threatening the destruction of large sections of Woolloomooloo, Darlinghurst, Kings Cross, Taylor Square and Bondi Junction. Although small sections of each freeway were constructed, both projects were abandoned in 1977. Other major national freeways, such as the M1 Pacific motorway from Sydney to Newcastle, were held up for months. In March 1974, in an astonishing display of strength, a mass meeting of Builders Labourers in Sydney banned all demolition work for the construction of expressways, in protest against the government's Nielsen Transportation Plan.

In Victoria, opposition to new freeways was part of a broader workers' campaign around pollution and public transport. The North Ballarat Railway Workshops Combined Unions Committee criticised the Bolte government's transport plan in 1970. Like his Liberal counterpart in NSW, Bolte prioritised development of new freeways at the expense of public transport. The committee concluded that a freeway system was not the answer to transport needs, and that the government was acting in the interests of freighting and automotive companies. The government plan would cause greater congestion on the roads and enormous pollution, with the automotive, oil and steel conglomerates the major beneficiaries. The Jolimont Workshops Committee declared that 'freeways ... at the behest of rubber-oil-concrete monopolies are not the answer to Melbourne's transport needs.'[122] The Preston Workshop Shop Committee had held public seminars in March 1969 to discuss the public transport system. The Newcastle AMWU branch, in an article on public transport, stressed that

> organisations of the people, trade unions (the Builders Labourers are already doing good work on this in Sydney) ... must today look at any of their problems ... Because, what use are bigger wages, better education, etc., if you drop dead from environmental stress.[123]

This was a new area of activity for unionists, one that put them far ahead of many of the politicians who were officially in charge of governing in the public interest.

Several unions banned work on an effluent pipeline in Townsville which was projected to dump four million gallons of industrial waste per day into Halifax Bay. Company-commissioned research claimed that no harm would come to people or marine life. A demand by a delegation of unionists and environmentalists that the research be made available to independent scrutiny was rejected. A meeting of AMWU members at the Yubulu Nickel treatment plant called for a black ban, which was made official by the Townsville T&LC in September 1974. The ban was to remain in place indefinitely – until the studies were released, but also until exemptions from prosecution under the Clean Water Act, given to the company by the Bjelke-Petersen government, were lifted. The circumstances under which the ban was lifted, or perhaps broken, remain unclear. In May 1975, after only three weeks of effluent discharge, independent marine studies found significant increases of mercury and other heavy metals in the bay near the outlet.

Union incursions into political and social affairs during the 1970s were an important part of the radical unionism of the period. AMWU organiser Ed Micaleff responded in an interview with *Link* to criticisms that his union was overstepping its responsibilities. His remarks demonstrate the radical nature of political unionism during the period:

> the Medibank stoppage … penal clauses' struggle … workers' compensation … that's a political issue. The Arbitration court is set up by a political act. Your whole life is politics … We have a right to say as much as a politician who is elected once every three years … in some cases, trade unions represent a larger proportion of the community than an elected government. On some issues, a more democratic perspective is being put by organised trade unions than a minority, gerrymandered elected government.

In his view, unions were more than just industrial bargaining organisations concerned with wages and conditions. They were important features of democratic political life. Such an attitude challenges the deep problems that representative democracies have with *participation*. As the major employer associations argued (see below), the trade union movement in the 1970s expressed what they perceived to be a popular dissatisfaction with parliamentary democracy, where political participation was reduced to voting every four years and waiting for the outcome. Instead, unions took direct action. In some cases, these actions were supported by large numbers in the unions and the general public; in others, they were the initiative of a small number of unionists and community members. The small actions are just as important as the large. If a small, working-class housing community can't take action to save their own community from a rapacious property developer, it is likely that no one else will.[124]

Union action around political questions continued into the later 1970s, although, with the large-scale decline in shop committees, direct action increasingly gave way to official gestures. The later 1970s were characterised by a rising cynicism toward parliamentary politics among many unionists, even as extra-parliamentary political action continued and increased. The dismissal of the Whitlam government was no doubt a factor in the tendency, resulting as it did in many ALP supporters losing faith in the ability of the party to effect change for workers through parliament. A 1977 industrial relations study observed that 'unionism is becoming more concerned with political questions', while 'the most distinctive form of union political activity among Australian unions is showing some signs of atrophy' – referring to support for the ALP. There is 'now a large body of evidence ... that most unionists do not approve of the affiliation of their unions to a party.' It is likely that, as well as a certain disillusionment with parliamentary avenues for change, many workers felt that their unions could be trusted to effect political change, where the parliamentary system perhaps could not.

CHAPTER 8
Crisis, Repression and Decline

THE BOSSES HIT BACK

Radical trade unionism in Australia gradually declined from the mid-1970s. Growing unemployment was a significant factor. As thousands of workers lost their jobs, a sort of chill began to settle over unionised workers, taking away their confidence and enthusiasm for radical action. The economy finally slipped into recession in late 1974, and economic conditions remained weak for the rest of the decade. The crisis was most severe in manufacturing, compounded by foreign imports and then offshoring. In an attempt to manage the crisis, the Whitlam government reduced tariffs on foreign imports, which many employers used as a justification for laying off workers. In manufacturing, where shop committees were strongest, some 200,000 jobs were lost between 1974 and 1984. John Halfpenny remarked in December 1974 that there had been some struggles against sackings, but:

> none of them have been very successful ... if you measure success in terms of preventing sackings from taking place. This is something of a new feature as compared to other periods. In 1971, for example, we were able to mount quite an offensive, and able to prevent the workers from being sacked in some cases, and in others to reduce the number. Some of the recent struggles have gone over a period

> of weeks, but none of them really achieved the result of preventing sackings … In 1971 we also had the dual problem of inflation and unemployment. What is different today is the magnitude of these problems.[125]

This opened the way for a direct assault on unions, as layoffs became a way for employers to more easily target union militants. The new radicalism of trade unions in the early 1970s was a source of deep consternation for employers, especially among the corporate lobby groups and large employer associations. Jack Mundey's quip to the 1973 Workers' Control Conference that the very notion of workers' control 'struck fear into the hearts of the employing class' was all too accurate.

Union activists were not only sacked, but many were also blacklisted from other employment. In one of several cases reported by *Link*, Jim Cowling, an AMWSU shop steward at Dunlop Bayswater, was dismissed in late 1976. Unable to find work despite 20 years of experience in the aircraft industry, he argued that that 'bosses are saying that if workers become militant, they'll be fired and won't get another job in the area,' pointing to blacklisting of shop stewards at Everhot, Vulcan and Insulwool in 1974. A large Melbourne-based maintenance shop owned by IPEC repeatedly targeted shopfloor activists, culminating in the dismissal of one AMWSU shop steward for 'theft and receiving stolen property' in 1978, despite a police investigation clearing him. Workers were unanimous that the whole incident was a 'set up job' that 'stank to high hell.' When they threatened strike action, a senior manager of the company travelled from Sydney to warn workers that the entire shop would be closed down if the action continued. In the context of the time, threats like these were often enough to avert industrial action.[126]

Employers were sometimes able to dismantle entire shop committees through layoffs. Kenworth Trucks in Melbourne dismissed 280 of its workers and the entire shop committee in October 1976, including the militant stewards and almost all AMWU members in the shop. They then locked out all remaining workers and notified the Commonwealth Employment Service that the workers were on strike and should not receive unemployment benefits. In October 1978, the APM Botany Mill in NSW succeeded in sacking large numbers of its workers and closing down a section of its operations, despite immediate strike action by its workers and the first nationwide stoppages at paper manufacturers. Despite this, the company sacked most of the leaders of the Combined Unions Committee.

A 1976 survey of metal manufacturers concluded that some companies 'were able to eliminate extra-militant or troublesome employees in the course of retrenchment' and that 'while the retrenchment process was often difficult ... it was ordinarily followed by a period of quieter relations in the plant.'[127]

Employer associations played a significant role in encouraging companies to undermine their unionised workforces. From 1971, business associations started large-scale public relations campaigns directed at employees, but also at schools, universities and the general public. They also joined together in confronting unions in industrial action. The Chamber of Commerce and Industry was most active, rivalled only by the American Chamber of Commerce in Australia and the major industry associations; other influential organisations included the Confederation of Australian Industry, Enterprise Australia, and think tanks like the Institute for Public Affairs and the Committee for Economic Development of Australia. Perhaps they were influenced by the publication in 1971 by Louis Powell, president of the Chambers of Commerce in the US, of the Powell Memorandum, which called for business to actively defend itself from trade unions and popular social movements.

Events at West Footscray Engineering are reflective of the change. When an AMWU shop steward was dismissed in 1975, a three-week strike by AMWU members at the plant won his reinstatement. In 1978, AMWSU members struck over a wage claim, and the company attempted to break picket lines by using trucks driven by scab drivers armed with crowbars. Union members responded by lying in front of the trucks and parking cars in front of the factory. Shop stewards ordered the manager to unload the trucks and, when the manager refused, workers imprisoned the trucks (which were rentals). The Victorian Chamber of Manufacturers then intervened directly; the AMWSU shop steward and the convenor of the shop committee were dismissed, earlier commitments to consider the wage claims were withdrawn, and the dispute was taken to arbitration. The outcome was no wage rise and failure to reverse any of the dismissals. The editors of *Link* speculated that management had been close to capitulating when the Chamber of Manufacturers had 'guaranteed that it would take care of lost company orders if it decided to hold out.' The editors further estimated that the company lost $3 million during the dispute and noted that this 'makes one wonder at the type and amount of pressure being put on it' by the employer association.[128]

In some cases, right wing union leaders helped employers to remove rank-and-file activists causing trouble in their industries. Large car industry employers pursued an offensive against shop committees from the mid-1970s, with support from VBEF officials. At the GM-Holden Elizabeth plant, members of the militant combined-union shop committee found themselves targeted for sacking. Ron Carli, a left wing VBEF activist, was 'locked out of the union' at GMH Fisherman's Bend by 1980 – the union officials refused to renew his membership, and he was not able to participate in meetings. As rank-and-file militancy fell away, hastened by the decline in shopfloor organisations, decisions within many unions were increasingly made by the leadership rather than the rank and file. The AMWSU – which incorporated every metal union by the end of the decade – tended increasingly toward corporatism and bureaucracy in the 1980s, characterised by a concentration of power in union officials and unelected bureaucrats, higher membership dues, and bargaining involving centralised political deals by senior officials. This model of unionism accompanied the introduction of the Prices and Incomes Accord between the ALP and the ACTU in the early 1980s, which in turn increased the tendency towards more corporatised union structures.

BLF DEREGISTRATION AND OTHER DEFEATS

Without a doubt, the major blow to radical trade unionism was the deregistration of the NSWBLF in 1974. The Arbitration Commission began deregistration proceedings against the union on behalf of the Master Builders Association in June. Norm Gallagher and other leaders of the national union actively colluded with employers, supported deregistration and took over the NSW branch. Norm Gallagher, national president, had a chequered history. He was far from unpopular and had been previously been a progressive figure within the union movement. In February 1971, thousands of BLF members stopped work in Melbourne and Brisbane in protest at his jailing for allegedly assaulting a developer during a dispute over a green ban in Carlton. Over a thousand workers attended a meeting in Festival Hall to demand his immediate release, and delegates of the rebel unions declared full support. Gallagher actively supported green bans.

Gallagher's support for deregistration of the NSWBLF was bitterly condemned by rank-and-file union members as a sell-out to property developers and the state and an attack on the existing direct democracy. Gallagher refused to speak at a single meeting during his six months in Sydney in 1974. Workers in NSW were forced to join the federal branch, and workers carrying old union tickets were sacked. Two dozen new state organisers were appointed, many of whom had been unsuccessful candidates in the 1973 election. Under the new regime, federal organisers had no obligation to hold branch meetings, stopwork meetings or even elections. FEDFA members who refused to work with federal BLF members had their wages cut and overtime banned. When FEDFA members struck over the issue, federal BLF leaders flew in crane drivers from Victoria to break the strike.

Unemployment lay beneath the surface of conflict. Green bans were locking up potential employment at a time when builders' labourers began to need it desperately. Federal members were happy to take work, and NSWBLF members no doubt confronted their options – fight to save their union or protect their own livelihoods in an economic recession. Gradually, solidarity was eroded. The state office was vandalised and robbed in March 1975, the organisation was criminalised and outcast, and the green bans were systematically broken and abandoned.

The malaise brought on by economic conditions and targeted sackings affected other unions into the later 1970s. The powerful shop committee at Ajax-Nettlefold, where retrenchments had been successfully resisted throughout 1977, was weakened after the retrenchment of 200 workers in 1978. Following an announcement of retrenchment of over 200 workers

Noticeboard at Sanyo TV factory Wodonga during sit-in 1978.
Photo courtesy Janey Stone.

at Sunshine and Ballarat, overtime bans were applied, but they were only partially supported by workers at other Ajax-Nettlefold factories. The AMWSU steward noted:

> if they had stuck together, if Richmond and Nunawading had supported Sunshine and Ballarat, they possibly could have continued to avoid the mass of retrenchments.

But the workers, exhausted by the bitter struggles of 1977, resigned themselves to the layoffs in the hope that they could simply win better terms of severance. A few weeks later, workers at a Sanyo plant in Albury–Wodonga staged a ten-day occupation to resist the retrenchment of about one in six of their workforce. Sanyo workers – almost all women – slept in the canteen for ten days to avoid lockout, holding daily meetings, even continuing aspects of work, in a late example of self-management for the period. By the time the company agreed to reverse retrenchments, the retrenched workers left the occupation and voluntarily resigned. The reversal of the company position suggests that the occupation had the potential to be successful, but demoralisation and hopelessness resulting from the prospect of likely unemployment became obstacles to militancy.

In spite of the decline, well-documented workplace occupations occurred in resistance to layoffs at Altona Petrochemical Complex (Melbourne) in 1979, and at two BHP mines in NSW in 1980. Waterfront unions continued to lead struggles, although action increasingly took the form of fundraising or statements of solidarity, such as with Polish workers during the early 1980s or in opposition to the Israeli invasion of Lebanon; stoppages and bans were less common. On the waterfront, just as in manufacturing, unemployment had a chilling effect. Rapid technology change had resulted in job losses over the course of the 1970s; the number of registered WWF members dropped by half in the ten years before 1977. The campaign against uranium mining, although not entirely ineffective, reflected a change in the strength of the labour movement. In 1977, the ACTU demanded that the Fraser government hold a referendum on uranium mining, to no avail. Some unions considered bans, but most unions were involved in uranium mining by 1979. The attitude of Charlie Fitzgibbon, former general secretary of the WWF, was perhaps representative of many:

> I would recommend to waterside workers that if other unions face up to their responsibility we will do likewise, but we will not be the fall guys.[129]

The spectre of unemployment meant that industrial action had become a kind of self-sacrifice, one that fewer workers were willing to make.

WAGE INDEXATION AND GOVERNMENT SUPPORT FOR EMPLOYERS' ATTACKS

Federal and state governments intervened in industrial relations in different ways throughout the 1970s. On the whole, their efforts were directed to reducing and undermining the strength of organised labour, either through direct repression or by coopting players in order to defuse militant union activism. Perhaps the 1975 introduction of federal wage indexation, according to which the Arbitration Commission was supposed to increase wages in line with prices and inflation, was the most effective strategy for constraining independent union activism. Wage indexation all but prohibited workplace wage bargaining, completely undermining the over-award campaigns that had been crucial to the development of militant trade unionism. Workers largely complied with federal wage guidelines, which led to a period of industrial inertia; from this, in some ways, the union movement never recovered.

It is easy to see how trade unionists bought into the policy of wage indexation. It promised that wages would increase with prices, which in turn served as the kind of price control that many, particularly on the left, had been demanding in response to inflation. Wage indexation would, in theory, remove the need for workers to strike for higher wages and improved conditions, handing the responsibility for negotiations over to paid officials and the state. Workers would not have to lose pay in strikes or deal with the bitter conflict that often accompanies industrial action. Unions were already on the back foot as a result of large-scale unemployment, and the lower success rate of strikes no doubt led many to view wage indexation as a more favourable alternative.

Yet, wage indexation – and its more significant continuation in the form of the Prices and Incomes Accord in the 1980s – was disastrous for rank-and-file trade unionism. *Link* noted that, at metal shops throughout Victoria, wage indexation had made it 'virtually impossible to organise successful shop floor action' and was almost certainly 'introduced as a means to *control* trade unions.'[130] Some efforts were made to oppose the policy. In the metal trades, for example, mass meetings of shop stewards called on the ACTU to abandon indexation, but the campaign had little impact. As left wing unionists warned, the core concept of indexation was that rank-and-file union members would hand over responsibility for wages and conditions in their workplaces to full-time officials and experts who could negotiate on their behalf. The radical trade unionism of the early 1970s was based on one idea more than any other: that ordinary workers had the right to make decisions about their own working lives, and unions were only the mechanism to enable this right. Giving up on this principle spelt the beginning of the end for radical unionism. It paved the way for the Accord in the 1980s, which in turn heralded an all-out employer offensive against the union movement.

Some roots of this retreat can be traced in earlier developments. Many left wing unionists greeted the election of a Labor government in 1972 as a victory for workers and argued that industrial unrest should be limited, to ensure that Labor remained in office. During the debate over union action to oppose Australian involvement in Vietnam, a *Tribune* reporter expressed exasperation that:

> Sure enough, in the Labour Council debate, Mr. J. Gibson (Glassworkers), who supported the executive's recommendation [to leave political issues to the ACTU], gave the banal cry that unions 'shouldn't embarrass the Labor Government.' How many more times will that be heard from right-wingers from now on, whenever unions are moving into effective action?

However, the Whitlam government itself acted to bring the union movement to heel. It blocked a wage campaign by airline pilots, established a Royal Commission to investigate the Seamen's Union and made strikers ineligible for the unemployment benefit. As we have seen, this last policy was quickly used by Kenworth Trucks to break a major strike over retrenchments in 1976. *Tribune* was right to oppose restraint in support of the Labor government. In the end, Whitlam was sacked anyway, and the attitudes of those who put their faith in the state to provide for workers translated neatly into support for wage indexation.[131]

Federal and state governments also ratcheted up legal support for employers who wanted to smash unions. The Liberal government of Dick Hamer in Victoria passed the *Vital Projects Act*, which created heavy fines for boycotts of vital state projects such as power stations. Bob Hawke described the act as 'the most repressive in Australia's history.' ECCUDO, the radical shop committee network in the NSW power industry, was broken after a 1975 campaign to introduce the 35-hour week, when the State government threatened them with massive fines. The militancy of

ECCUDO faded after 1975, and they abandoned the struggle for 35-hours.

Federal legislation to control trade unions expanded dramatically under Malcolm Fraser, including establishment of the Industrial Relations Bureau and the outlawing of secondary boycotts in 1977, and amendments to the Conciliation and Arbitration Act in 1979. Other legislation allowed the Federal government to arbitrarily dismiss any government worker taking industrial action. Ron Carrington, a delegate to the Australian Government Establishments Shop Committee, described the feelings of concern among his members and called the legislation 'another union bashing bill and one with no right of appeal.'[132] The government did avoid an attempt to smash unions through a direct confrontation, fearing it would result in a repeat of the 1969 penal powers affair. Some smaller-scale confrontations, such as that between the Western Australian government and the AMWSU in 1979, did result in a backdown by the state. Unions themselves were no longer confident of their ability to win major set-piece battles, even if governments feared that they could.

WORKERS' PARTICIPATION REPLACES WORKERS' CONTROL

Large employers and their associations began to promote 'worker participation' schemes, consisting of consultative management techniques, autonomous work projects, job enrichment and employee communications programs characteristic of modern human resources management. Such programs were designed to come between workers and their unions by promoting company-controlled mechanisms for decision making and involvement. Participating workers could belong to unions, but they were not union structures. Sociologist Harvie Ramsay argues in the British context that workers' participation schemes 'are shown to correspond to periods when management authority is felt to be facing challenge' and are 'thus best understood as a means of attempting to secure labour's compliance', as opposed to a genuine democratisation of industry. Australian militants were wary of the dangers posed by 'worker participation' from the outset. In its invitations to the initial 1969 Workers' Control Conference, the CPA warned that:

> In other countries the movement [for workers' control] tended to be 'bought off' by phoney schemes of participation and profit sharing as a substitute for effective control by workers which actually limits controls exercised by employers.

In other words, workers would be allowed to participate through management-designed tools but would give up genuine control as their unions fell away.

It is important to recognise that workers' control was vulnerable to cooption by employers from the start. Frank Bollins, metal unionist and prominent CPA member, warned in 1969 that 'dangers of class collaboration and integration would be ever present in worker control' in the form of 'merging interests of employer and worker.' He argued that there was a risk that workers organised in shop and site committees with *some* independence from trade unions might eventually become completely separated from unions to become organs within the companies. This was exactly the idea behind worker participation schemes and their later iterations in the form of human resources management.[133]

Employers' intentions for worker participation schemes were quite clear. The Central Industrial Secretariat, the giant employers' association formed in 1973, warned in a document called *Industry and Society* in that year that 'society seems to have reached a point where the individual is no longer prepared to wait to express pleasure or displeasure at social events and decisions at the ballot box', and 'strikes, black bans and other types of industrial action are being used as a mechanism for the resolution of social differences.' There was, therefore, a need for 'containing these expressions of concern within a socially and politically acceptable framework.' The organisation proposed 'worker participation' as the kind of 'acceptable framework' that would work to restore democracy to a more manageable expression. Another document, *Communication, Consultation, Negotiation*, emphasises the need for more 'human' managerial styles, based around direct company contact with workers to 'take its employees behind the decisions' made by management, with the caveat that 'this does not mean the abandoning or sharing of management's right and responsibility of decision making.' In similar terms, a Liberal Party pamphlet that decried 'the muzzling and control of management by worker committees' in 1973 offered one clear solution: worker participation schemes that would:

> eliminate these situations by taking a responsible attitude to the man on the shop floor and giving him the opportunity to add his voice to the success and productivity of the company.

For the Liberal Party, this was 'the most effective way of limiting industrial disputes while at the same time negating the insidious doctrine of workers' control.' Even Malcom Fraser himself, who hated unions, wrote of 'the need for those who work in an industry to have a sense of participation, involvement and responsibility.'[134]

Widespread enthusiasm for participation circulated within professional management circles. Walter Scott concluded his 'communication gap' speech (discussed in Chapter 1) to Australian managers by advising that: 'the one already well formulated possibility which gives some ray of hope and which may grow and expand rapidly during the 1970s is participation.' In 1977, the AIM explained that:

> four reasons are most often advanced in Australia to support worker participation. The most popular by far is: With increasing education and affluence employees will no longer happily work in jobs which are monotonous and meaningless.

It added: 'something must be done to improve the relationship between employer and employee because of the cost and disruption due to industrial disharmony.' In sum, employers and managers were arguing that the tendency towards independent workers' control by shop committees could be negated by allowing workers a sense of autonomy in their work, carefully controlled by management. A survey of 140 managers belonging to the AIM in 1978 concluded that 'worker participation techniques that threaten neither managerial prerogative nor profits are widely favoured by the managers.'[135]

American-based multinationals were eager proponents of new management techniques. GM-Holden introduced worker participation programs and human resource management to its Australian plants in the mid-1970s. Ron Carli notes that large numbers of workers were 'cynical' about 'autonomous work groups', in which workers did not have strong managerial oversight, and Carli himself refused to participate in them. He was sceptical of the company's constant attempts to communicate with workers and ensure their wellbeing. As he saw it, he and others were 'not too happy to accept the idea that we've got to work collaboratively with management', quite simply because he was 'brought up in Communist ideology.' The VBEF shop committee at the Tonsley Park Chrysler plant in Adelaide voted to reject a workers' participation scheme in 1974, with the support of their officials. *Tribune* reported:

> This rejection by Chrysler workers of Joint Consultation Committees is a good start in fighting these class collaborationist ideas. Workers and shop stewards in all factories, notably the vehicle building industry, should take this as a lead and publicise it widely. It shows that the false turning proposed by Dunstan and Co. for the workers' movement can be avoided if the groundwork is laid beforehand.

The article further points to 'the raising of consciousness about the issue' by the Workers' Control Centre, which had recently sent a leaflet on joint consultation committees to shop committees.[136] Shopfloor militants and radical unionists were thus often able to help workers understand the role of worker participation. In other enterprises, these schemes were embraced by workers who were unaware of their employers' intentions.

By such processes, shop committees were separated from the trade unions and incorporated into management systems. One instance was early in 1977, when the AMWSU steward and shop committee convenor at B&D Doors expressed concern that the committee was becoming a management tool to placate the workforce and undermine militancy. They claimed that:

> the company doesn't recognise the shop committee as a union meeting, they believe the committee's only for the purpose of identifying small problems on the shop-floor, it makes it easier for them.

The shop committee expressed frustration that management was:

> always put[ting] responsibility onto the workers to do things like setting up a new canteen, investigate cooling systems for the place, chose [sic] the colour paint for the toilets

After blockades occurred at Draffin-Everhot in resistance to retrenchments, management *suggested* the formation of a workers' committee to improve communication. After the series of bans and sit-ins imposed by AMWU members at IMCO Containers in Ferntree Gully (discussed above in **Job Control**), *Link* reported that 'all the supervisors and top management have been sent off to school to learn about "industrial relations".'[137] In this way, management was able to use the relative autonomy of shop committees to coopt and undermine them.

Many trade unions were critical of participation schemes, because they were intended to separate members from their unions and coopt them into management-controlled systems. The AMWU had a policy against participation.. John Halfpenny, as president of the union, described workers' participation as 'little short of management-labour co-operation for the achievement of management objectives' and:

> channelling the ever-increasing demand of workers for greater involvement in the work and decision-making processes into more respectable channels which pose less of a threat to management power.

CHAPTER 8: CRISIS, REPRESSION AND DECLINE 155

Instead, he expressed support for 'worker involvement which produces greater interference and intervention through independent trade union organisation rather than through participation' and 'greater involvement in the work place and in society.' A Queensland Workers' Control Conference paper in November 1973 rejected efforts by employers and governments to 'counter the idea of workers' control with the more moderate idea of "workers' participation"', described as 'putting a worker on a board of representatives where he or she is outnumbered by bosses' representatives.' The AIM conceded that 'there is perhaps greater hostility and suspicion towards the concept of worker participation in the Trade Union movement than in industrial and commercial management circles', and that 'where unions do show interest, they invariably equate increased worker participation with increased union participation.' AIM also excoriated what it argued was the intention of left wing trade unionists :

> to use worker participation as a tactic in causing the collapse of the present political and economic system and the destruction of the institution of private ownership.[138]

In some enterprises, unions and managers fought bitterly over the nature of participation. Upon hearing union proposals for a scheme in 1976, management at ICI Botany 'launched into an attack on the "workers' control" concepts in the proposals, and the presence of the Union Secretary.' AMWU members believed that the scheme 'severely limited the amount of control the rank and file would have over the projects' and 'gave up in disgust.' Workers' control was a living issue at ICI: the Combined Shop committee at ICI Osborne in SA, for example, had waged a campaign to gain access to the company's financial records.

Graeme Watson believes that a participation scheme was introduced at a power depot in Oakleigh (Melbourne), precisely because it was a militant stronghold and thorn in the side of the SEC. He recalls that:

> in about 1972 ... my depot—the Oakleigh Area Centre—I was the shop steward there, [was] very heavily unionised,

> very militant depot. It was decided that this would be the place that they would trial industrial democracy ... I always wondered, why Oakleigh? And maybe it was to try to shut me down or whatever, I'm not sure.

Watson recalls further that the SEC 'wouldn't dare try it inside the La Trobe Valley'; that was one of the most powerful union sites, and they would never have succeeded.[139]

On the whole, workers' participation schemes were intended as a way for employers to undermine independent union organisation in their workplaces. The industrial relations scholar Harry Braverman perhaps captured the point best, describing worker participation as:

> a gracious liberality in allowing the worker to adjust a machine, replace a light bulb, move from one fractional job to another, and they have the illusion of making decisions by choosing among fixed and limited alternatives designed by management which deliberately leaves insignificant matters open to choice.

Participation schemes, while giving an illusion of worker independence and control, were insidious in their erosion of both. The faddishness with which they were embraced by employers in the mid-1970s waned later, when mass unemployment and targeted dismissals became more effective means of dealing with militant trade unions. Human resources management, however, built on more or less the same principles, has become the norm.[140]

CHAPTER 9
Radical Legacies

The radical workers' struggles of the 1970s were undermined, smashed, eroded and marginalised before they could achieve lasting systemic change. Since that decade, unions have been pushed to the margins of economic affairs, and progressive struggles to advance new frontiers of workers' power have given way to defensive actions to preserve trade unions themselves. Australian workers, despite making up most of the population, remain dependent on a tiny minority of political decision makers and a wealthy elite. The same obstacles that were so effective in undermining workers' control in the 1970s – unemployment, repression, new ways of managing labour and others – have become deliberate, structural features of neoliberal economies. Discussion of a green ban on the proposed East West Link freeway (Melbourne) prior to the project's demise in November 2014 was ultimately muted by demands for employment. The vast majority of working people have little or no control over the places where they spend the majority of their lives, and no control over the economic institutions that dictate many aspects of their lives beyond work. The dictatorship of 'the boss' is stable.

However, this book shows that, when workers are given the opportunity to challenge or even replace the authority of their bosses with a more democratic alternative, the decision to do so comes more easily than might be expected. Many experiments with workers' control are characterised by a certain urge for freedom from managerial control, even where the likelihood of any lasting success is minimal. We can connect this to a deeper impulse. As one historian puts it, workers' control 'reflects no more than the capacity of all humans to think as well as to do', and 'it should not be surprising that workers on occasion take over and run productive enterprises without necessarily having an explicit consciousness or political strategy', because the 'faculties they draw upon for such initiatives are not so much new as they are long suppressed.'[141]

The same might be said about workers' willingness to confront the state. The union movement demonstrated enormous power in its defeat of the penal powers in 1969. Not only did mass strike action render the laws ineffective, but subsequent strikes ensured that they stayed a dead letter. On several occasions, the threat of mass strike action forced the state to release arrested union representatives. Ordinary union members were at the core of these actions. Victorian BLF leader John Cummins pointed out at a seminar of unionists, in July 1993, that the penal powers strikes weren't called by the ACTU. In fact, the Victorian Trades Hall Council advised union members that they were in no way obliged to participate in 'unauthorised stoppages', because this was 'contrary to the rules, procedures and decisions of the ACTU.'[142] Cummins went on to say that this struggle reinforced his view that:

> if we are to build fighting unions, then don't look to Trades Hall or the ACTU for a solution. My experience over the years is that there's no problem with workers taking action: it's the leadership that's needed. And that's the issue we've got to fix.

Corey Oakley writes:

> The rising levels of industrial militancy in the late 1960s were driven much more by an upheaval from below than by the trade union leadership.[143]

While rank-and-file activism was the decisive factor, supportive union leaders were also important. In the left wing unions particularly, union leaderships were responsive to, and respected by, their members.

CHAPTER 9: RADICAL LEGACIES   159

Workers' control struggles did not disappear at the end of the 1970s. Where enterprises and industries retain high levels of union organisation, or where radicals have managed to introduce militant and innovative tactics to real struggles, the spirit of the earlier actions has lived on. In the first two months of 1990, Melbourne tram operators, led by the Anarcho-Syndicalist Federation, operated trams for free in opposition to the removal of tram conductors. At one point, there were worker occupations at the Brunswick, Essendon, Kew, North Fitzroy, Preston and South Melbourne tram depots. A banner at the Brunswick Depot read in bold: 'This Depot Under Workers' Control'. Sit-ins and occupations continue to occur sporadically even to the present day. In July 2014, members of the Rail, Tram and Bus Union obstructed train lines to press for reinstatement of a dismissed worker. In early 2015, a protracted factory occupation over wages and conditions occurred at International Flavours and Fragrances in Dandenong (Melbourne).

The Earthworker Cooperative has been establishing worker-owned and worker-directed enterprises in Victoria, using a broad network of trade unions and public institutions to ensure 'collective markets' for their goods and services. The project is described by its spokesperson, Dave Kerin, who belonged to both the BLF and CPA in the 1970s, as:

> developing a new economic space—at the heart of it is democratic ownership. Trade unions are a form of workers' power that exists currently, and they will be important to growing the power of people and workers in the future.[144]

In 2018, Earthworker helped to launch the Redgum Cleaning Cooperative, another worker-owned firm in an industry where worker cooperatives have flourished internationally. As recently as 2017, the Construction, Forestry, Maritime, Mining and Energy Union (CFMEU) imposed a green ban on the redevelopment of Sydney's historic Bondi Pavilion. While this was touted as an art deco renovation, its opponents were concerned that it was really designed to privatise public space. Famous NSWBLF figure, Jack Mundey, joined CFMEU members in announcing the action. Workers' control over health and safety is now a part of the collaborative frameworks introduced in the 1980s, and the ongoing leadership of unions in this area speaks to the legacy of the 1970s.

Australia in the 1970s looked very different to the Australia of today. The earlier period represented a high point of trade union organisation and industrial militancy. Unprecedented gains were won by ordinary trade union members. Short lived though many of them were, they resulted in huge improvements in the lives of ordinary people. Radical union action moved from the margins to somewhere near the centre of industrial and political life.

Chronically low rates of union membership in the present have led some to suggest that unions are beyond salvation. It is easy to believe that contemporary unions have become so mired in bureaucracy and corporatism that they cannot possibly serve as democratic instruments for radical social change. But a democratic trade union movement led by rank-and-file union members is absolutely vital to any sort of progressive future. Workers' control in the 1970s was based firstly around organisation of workers at the workplace, then connected to communities, trade union leadership and other supports. Although much of what happened during the 1970s appeared spontaneous, it was only possible because of decades of hard work by committed union activists. These foundations can be built again, and there is no time like the present.

ENDNOTES

Chapter 1

1. T Bramble, 'Managers of discontent', in Rick Kuhn (ed.), *Class and Struggle in Australia*, Pearson Education Australia, 2005, p.

2. T. Bramble, 'Managers of discontent', p.

3. K. Coates and T. Topham, *The New Unionism: The Case for Workers' Control*, London, Peter Owens, 1972, p. 6.

4. Many quotes from people directly involved in actions around workers' control come from interviews which I conducted and recorded personally. The quotes cannot otherwise be referenced.

5. J. Hutson, 'Workers Control', *Australian Left Review*, no. 1, February–March 1969, p. 8.

6. 'Symposium: Workers' Control', *Australian Left Review*, no. 41, August 1973, p. 12.

7. C. L. Goodrich, *The Frontier of Control: A Study in British Workshop Politics*, 2nd edn, London, Pluto Press, 1975, p. 18.

8. G. Souter, 'Sacking the boss: from "working-in" to taking over', *Sydney Morning Herald*, 28 July 1973.

9. K. Murphy, 'ALP president says "deep crisis" in unions must be addressed', *The Guardian*, 2 February 2018.

10. S.P. Huntington, M.J. Crozier, and J. Watanuki, *The Crisis of Democracy: Report on the Governability of Democracies to the Trilateral Commission*, New York, Trilateral Commission & New York University Press, 1975.

11   C. Harman, *The Fire Last Time: 1968 and After*, 2nd edn, London, Bookmarks, 1998, p. 235.

12   Wildcat Dodge Truck 1974 [np].

13   H. S. Albinski, *Politics and Foreign Policy in Australia: The Impact of Vietnam and Conscription*, Durham, Duke University Press, 1970, pp. 208–9.

14   'Symposium: Workers' Control', *Australian Left Review*, no. 41, August 1973, p. 14.

15   'Young Workers in Revolt', *Tribune*, April 11–17, 1972, p. 7; H. Braverman, *Labour and Monopoly Capital: The Degradation of Work in the Twentieth Century*, New York & London, Monthly Review Press, 1974, p. 35.

Chapter 2

16   C. McGregor, *Profile of Australia*, London, Hodder & Stoughton, 1966, pp. 15, 93.

17   T. Bramble, *Trade Unionism in Australia: A History from Flood to Ebb Tide*, Port Melbourne, Cambridge University Press, 2008, p. 13.

18   Minutes of National Conference of Full-Time Officials, AEU Melbourne District Committee, November 1964, Box 1, 1987.0116, University of Melbourne Archives.

19   Quotes and statistics taken from T. Bramble, *Trade Unionism in Australia*.

20   A. E. Woodward, 'Industrial Relations in the 70s', *Journal of Industrial Relations* 12, no. 2, 1970, p. 124; Carmichael quote taken from Minutes of National Conference of Full-Time Officials, AEU Melbourne District Committee, November 1964, Box 1, 1987.0116, University of Melbourne Archives.

21   J. Halfpenny, 'V.B.F Finally Joins Dispute', *AEU Monthly Journal*, January 1970, p. 24; 'First Ethnic Shop Committee,' *Link: Western Suburbs*, March 1977.

22   Addresses, Reports and Decisions of the Second Commonwealth Conference, AEU Melbourne District Committee, 26 April–5 May 1971, Box 1, 1987.0116, University of Melbourne Archives; T. Bramble, 'Australian Trade Union Strategies since 1945,' *Labour and Industry*, vol. 11, no. 3, April 2001, p. 14; J Hutson, *Penal Colony to Penal Powers*,

Surry Hills, Amalgamated Engineering Union, 1966, pp. 217, 219.

23   'Strike Turmoil', *Sydney Morning Herald*, 23 September, 1971, p. 6.

24   C. Gifford, 'Gladstone: fight for rights on job', *Tribune*, 21–27 November 1972, p. 7.

25   Quoted in V. Burgmann and M. Burgmann, *Green Bans, Red Union: Environmental Activism and the New South Wales Builders Labourers' Federation*, Sydney, University of New South Wales Press, 1998, p. 100.

26   Jack Hutson, 'Workers Control', *Australian Left Review*, no. 1, February–March 1969, p. 12; Joe Palmada, 'Issues of industrial strategy', *Australian Left Review*, no. 31, July 1971, p. 2.

27   'Call to members for more involvement in union affairs,' *Labor News*, vol. 26, no. 191, September 1971, p. 8.

Chapter 3

28   Jack Hutson, 'Workers Control', *Australian Left Review*, no. 1, February-March 1969, p. 8; Denis Freney, 'Scope for workers' control,' *Tribune*, 17–23 April 1973, p. 5.

29   'Invites for workers' control forum go to factory reps', *Tribune*, 16 July 1969, p. 12; Quotes from *Australian Left Review* come from 'Workers' Control: A Symposium,' *Australian Left Review*, no. 2, April–May 1969, p. 8.

30   P. Thomas, 'Workers' control: A Modest Proposal', *Tribune*, 3 September 1969, p. 6.

31   D. Freney, 'Workers' Control Perspectives', *Australian Left Review*, no. 39, 1973, p. 3; Quotes from Owens and Lofthouse come from 'Symposium: Workers' Control', *Australian Left Review*, no. 41, August 1973.

32   D. Freney, 'Scope for workers' control', *Tribune*, 17–23 April 1973, p. 5.

33   See E. Roberts, *Workers' Control*, London, George Allen & Unwin, 1973, p. 44.

34   R. Arnold, 'Seeing Workers' Control in Belgrade', *Boilermakers – Blacksmiths Journal*, no. 19, June 1972, p. 5.

35   *Towards a Socialist Australia: How the labor movement can fight back. Documents of the Socialist Workers Party*, Sydney, Pathfinder Press, 1977, p. 102.

36 M. Schmidt and L. Van Der Walt, *Black Flame: The Revolutionary Class Politics of Anarchism and Syndicalism*, Oakland, CA, AK Press, 2009, p. 7; N. Chomsky, *Government in the Future*, New York, Seven Stories Press, 2005, 28–29. Based on a talk given at the Poetry Centre, New York City, 16 February 1970; C. Harman, *The Fire last time*, p. 235.

37 J. Hutson, 'Workers' Control', *Australian Left Review*, no. 1, February–March 1969, pp. 8–9; Melbourne Railway Rank and File Group, 'Workers' Control or Self-Management?' *Melbourne Anarchist Archives: development of Melbourne anarchism: drafts, documents & articles, 1966–1973*, [Melbourne?] ca. 1973, p. 87.

38 C. Oakley, 'The rise and fall of the ALP left in Victoria and NSW', *Marxist Left Review*, No 4, Winter 2012, p 63.

39 Cited in C. Oakley.

40 K. Wang, Unit for Industrial Democracy, 'Current Debate', paper presented to the Health Service Personnel Officers' First National Seminar, Adelaide, 26 March 1976.

41 Modern Unionism and the Workers' Movement. Communist Party of Australia, 22nd Congress, March 1970, Sydney, Red Pan Publications, 1970, p. 10; *A Strategy for the 1980s in the Metal Industry* [np], Communist Party of Australia, ca 1980, p. 11.

42 Quote from CPA conference 1972 taken from V. Burgmann and M. Burgmann, *Green Bans*, pp. 95–96; Quote from 1973 Workers' Control Group taken from 'On Workers' Control', *Tribune*, 13–19 June 1972, p. 11.

43 'Symposium: Workers' Control,' *Australian Left Review*, no. 41, August 1973, p. 13.

Chapter 4

44 C. Cameron, 'Managerial Control and Industrial Democracy: Myths and Realities,' address to the AIM, NSW Division President's Dinner, Sydney, 20 August 1973.

45 'What is Workers' Control?' Proceedings of the Queensland Workers' Control Conference, Brisbane, Waterside Workers' Club, November 1973; J. Moss, *Industrial Relations or Workers Control: South Australian Experiences*, Adelaide, People's Bookshop, 1973, p. 22.

46 J. Reed, 'Women work-in at BHP', *Tribune*, 10–16 April 1973, p. 5.

47   M. Derber, 'Changing Union-Management Relations at the Plant Level in Australian Metalworking', *The Journal of Industrial Relations*, vol. 19, No. 1, March 1977,, p. 15.

48   R. Dixon, '130,000 Workless by March', *Tribune*, 8 December 1971, p. 3; See also 'Action on sackings scores a victory', *Tribune*, 1 December 1971, p. 4.

49   'Police Arrest Work-In Men,' *Tribune*, 6–10 April 1973, p. 2.

50   'Metal Workers Occupy Balmain Job: Work-In to Stop Sackings', *Tribune*, 28 January 1975, p. 4.

51   R. Clark, 'Car worker Jailed for Refusing the Sack', *Direct Action*, 24 April 1975, p. 5.

52   Addresses, Reports and Decisions of the First Commonwealth Conference, AEU Melbourne District Committee, May 1969, Box 1, 1987.0116, University of Melbourne Archives.

53   P. Thomas, *Miners in the 1970s: A Narrative History of the Miners' Federation*, Sydney, Miners Federation, 1983, p. 54.

54   'Sack Boss Instead', *Tribune*, March 10, 1971, p. 10.

55   Quotes taken from V. Burgmann & M. Burgmann, *Green Bans, Red Union*, p. 97.

56   'Warning! Work is a Health Hazard', *Link*, September 1976.

57   'Workers Reject Settlement', *Link: Western Suburbs Metal Workers Bulletin*, August 1976.

58   *Tribune*, May 19, 1971.

59   Quoted in V. Burgmann and M. Burgmann, *Green Bans, Red Union*, p. 110.

60   Ted Gnatenko, in AMWU (ed.), *Talking Back: Reflections of Retired AMWU Activists*, Granville, NSW, AMWU, 2006, p. 98.

61   Ted Gnatenko, in AMWU (ed.), *Talking Back*, p. 99.

62   'Rail workers act on safety', *Tribune*, August 15–21, 1972, p. 4.

63   'Workers' Health in Workers' Hands', *Workers' Health*, no. 1, 1977.

64   Hazards: Bulletin of the Queensland Workers' Health Centre, no. 6, April 1982, p. 11.

65 *How to Look at Your Plant*, Sydney, Industrial Health Workers' Group, ca. 1977.

66 'Job control in theory and practice', *The Movement*, vol. 1, no. 8, August 1920. Reprinted in *Australian Left Review*, no. 35, 1972, p. 29.

67 *AEU–ASE–Springhill Maintenance –Fork Lift Trucks*, John Lysaght Ltd, Sheet Manufacturing Division, 11/1–11/5, 1970, John Lysaght Collection, D52, University of Wollongong Archives.

68 Political Research Group & Political Economy Movement, 'Workers, Trade Unions & Industrial Democracy', *Journal of Australian Political Economy*, vol. 3, 1978, p. 82; Central Industrial Secretariat, *Industry and Society*, [Canberra?] ca. 1974, p. 4.

69 AEU, *Monthly Journal*, April 1970, p. 30.

70 'Vehicle Industry Report', AMWU *Monthly Journal*, July 1973, p. 5; 'Victoria State Report', AMWU *Monthly Journal*, August 1973, p. 23; Sol Marks, in AMWU (ed.), *Talking Back*, p. 125.

71 Sol Marks, in AMWU (ed.), *Talking Back*, p. 124; C.L.R. James, with R. Dunayevskaya and G. Lee, *State Capitalism and World Revolution*, 2nd edn, Chicago, Charles H. Kerr, 1986, p. 42.

72 G. Phelan, 'Shop Floor Organisation: Some Experiences from the Vehicle Industry', *Australian Left Review*, no. 78, 1981, p. 10.

73 T. Topham, *Productivity Bargaining and Workers' Control*, [Nottingham?] Institute for Workers' Control, 1968, p. 1.

74 All quotes from 'Fighting Ford's Dictatorship', *Link*, November 1978.

75 M. Westcott, 'Worker Control in Oil Industry', *Labour & Industry*, pp. 406–407.

76 Frank Cherry quote from 'Workers sack boss at container plant', *Tribune*, 17 September 1974, p. 4; Goodrich, *Frontier of Control*, pp. 35, 18.

Chapter 5

77 M. Tubbs, 'Harco Men's Story', *Tribune*, no. 1712, 30 June 1971, p. 7.

78 M. Tubbs and B. Caldwell, *The Harco work-in: an experience of workers' control*, Sydney, Sydney Centre for Workers' Control, 1973, p. 1.

79 'The Workers Sacked the Boss,' *Tribune*, 1–7 February 1972, p. 4.

80 'The Workers Sacked the Boss.'

81 All quotes from J. Owens and J. Wallace, *Workers Call the Tune at Opera House*, Sydney, National Workers Control Conference, 1973.

82 'Workers "We'll Build It"', *Tribune*, 24 September 1974, p. 4.

83 'PWD strikers work-in on docks,' *Tribune*, May 1–7, 1973, p. 4.

84 'Workers Seize Site, Defy Cops,' *Tribune*, May 7-13, 1974, p. 1.

85 All quotes from P. Thomas, *Miners in the 1970s*, pp. 25, 26.

86 All quotes from P. Thomas, *Miners in the 1970s*, p. 28.

87 All quotes from P. Thomas, *Miners in the 1970s*, pp. 52, 53.

88 J. McIlroy, 'NSW Power Workers Vote to Drop Bans', *Direct Action*, no. 78, 7 February 1975, p. 5.

89 'Power workers in control', *Tribune*, 10–16 July 1973, p. 4; Gavin Souter, 'Sacking the boss: from "working-in" to taking over', *Sydney Morning Herald*, 28 July 1973; 'Cockle Creek', *Tribune*, 4 March 1975.

90 'Chemical workers action', *Tribune*, 12-19 March 1973, p. 4; 'How unions looked after the essential services,' *Tribune*, 8–14 August 1972.

91 'Chemical workers action,' *Tribune*, 12–19 March 1973, p. 4; 'How unions looked after the essential services', *Tribune*, 8–14 August 1972; 'Unions to free some oil', *The Herald*, 26 July 1972, p. 1.

92 'WORK-IN', *Link*, March 1978.

Chapter 6

93 M. Munro-Clark, *Communes in Rural Australia: The Movement since 1970*, Sydney, Hale and Iremonger, 1986, p. 14.

94 P. Thomas, *Miners in the 1970s*, p. 28.

95 Quotes from P. Thomas, *Miners in the 1970s*, pp. 37, 41.

96 All quotes from P. Thomas, *Miners in the 1970s*, pp. 43–45.

97 Quotes from this paragraph and that directly above are taken from V. Burgmann, R. Jureidini, and M. Burgmann, 'Doing Without the Boss: Workers' Control Experiments in Australia in the 1970s', *Labour History: A Journal of Labour and Social History*, vol. 103, 2012, p. 114.

98 'Greg Pettiona discusses attacks on militancy', *Link: Eastern Suburbs*, December 1974.

99   'PWD strikers work-in on docks', *Tribune*, May 1–7, 1973, p. 4.

100 As quoted in 'Bourke's store; red herring', *Tribune*, March 20–26, 1973, p. 4.

101 MUA, Commonwealth Shop Stewards Committee Victoria, Eric Persson's Papers, Resolutions Carried at Delegate and Mass Meetings, need ref number, Box 1, Meeting of Commonwealth Workers Resolution, 18 September 1973.

102 'Clydemaster: Workers Act to Secure Jobs', *Link: Eastern Suburbs*, May 1978.

Chapter 7

103 J. Moss, *Industrial Relations or Workers' Control: South Australian Experiences*, Adelaide, People's Bookshop, 1973, pp. 22, 5.

104 B. Creighton, 'Law and Control of Industrial Conflict', in K. Cole (ed.), *Power, conflict and control in Australian trade unions*, Ringwood, Pelican, pp. 130–131; A. Carey, *Taking the risk out of democracy: Propaganda in the US and Australia*, Sydney, University of New South Wales Press, 1995, p. 99.

105 Quotes from M. Beasley, *Wharfies: The History of the Waterside Workers' Federation*, Halstead Press/Australian National Maritime Museum, 1996, p. 218.

106 B. Dunnett, 'On the job organisation vital', *Tribune*, 17 February 1971, p. 7.

107 'Maritime Boycott', *Tribune*, 16–22 January 1973, p. 10.

108 'Trade Union Submission on the Proposed Omega Installation to Foreign Affairs Committee, Australian Parliament', *Dynamo*, Vol. 3, No. 3, August 1973, p. 6.

109 G. Mallory, *Uncharted Waters: Social Responsibility in Australian Trade Unions*, Annerley, QLD, Greg Mallory, 2005, p. 131.

110 'And the cargo stayed behind', *Tribune*, 2 June 1971, p. 4.

111 AMWU *Monthly Journal*, November 1975, p. 11; *The Age*, 9 June 1976, cited in T. O'Lincoln, *Years of Rage: Social Conflicts in the Fraser Era*, Melbourne, Bookmarks, 1993, p. 64; 'Rank and File Unity', *Link*, July 1976.

112 'Prices Protest', *Dynamo*, vol. 13, no. 3, August 1973, p. 13; N. McKenzie,

'What are we looking for when we say price control? *Newcastle Metal Worker*, vol. 1, no. 2, ca. 1972, p. 3; A. Robertson, 'Price Control needs Workers Control', *Tribune*, 3 February 1971, p. 5.

113 'Tony Vrettos & junta', *Tribune*, 26 August 1970.

114 'Bans hailed', *Tribune*, 29 January–4 February, 1974, p. 4.

115 M. Haskell, 'Green Bans: Worker Control and the Urban Environment', *Industrial Relations*, vol. 16, No. 2 (May 1977), pp. 209–210.

116 M. Haskell, 'Green Bans', p. 193.

117 'SA union and environment', *Tribune*, 23–29 May 1972, p. 4.

118 'The Dilemma of Port Phillip', *Tribune*, 26 February 1969, p. 4.

119 'Queensland Union's muscle in fight to save Barrier Reef', *Tribune*, 28 January 1970, p. 12; 'Unions reaching beyond bread & margarine issues', *Tribune*, 18 February 1970, p. 10.

120 'Roads—Pipes and Wires: A Union Viewpoint', AMWU *Monthly Journal*, pp. 18–19.

121 'The Industrial Front', *Tribune*, 7 April 1971, p. 10.

122 'Some Thoughts on Transport in Australia with Special Reference to Melbourne', Correspondence of the Jolimont Railway Workshops, 1968–1970, ca. 1969, Records of the Ballarat North Railway Workshops Inter-Union Shop Committee, Box 2, 1979.0159, University of Melbourne Archives.

123 'Transport and the Future: How it affects Newcastle', *The Newcastle Metal Worker: Official Organ of the AMWU Newcastle Branch*, vol. 1, no. 2, ca. 1972, p. 7.

124 D. Rawson, *Unions and Unionists in Australia*, Sydney, George Allen & Unwin, 1978, pp. 80, 91; 'Newport: Why is is Fraser so Determined?' *Link: North Western Suburbs*, December 1976.

Chapter 8

125 Interview with John Halfpenny, *RPM: Militant Workers' Bulletin*, no. 5, December, 1974, p. 6.

126 'Steward Blacklisted', *The Link: Eastern Suburbs*, September 1976; 'Company says . . . bugger the union', *Link*, June 1978.

127 M. Derber, 'Changing Union-Management Relations', p. 15.

128 'Chamber of Manipulators', *Link*, March 1978.

129 M. Beasley, *Wharfies*, p. 238.

130 'Indexation: Moore Rip Offs', *Link: Western Suburbs Metal Workers Bulletin*, March 1977.

131 C. Cameron, 'Industrial Disputes in Australia: The Correct Perspective,' address by Mr. Clyde R. Cameron, American Chamber of Commerce in Australia luncheon, Melbourne, 30 November 1973; 'Rightwing & unions' ban', *Tribune*, 23–29 January 1973, p. 12.

132 'Right to Strike: New Threat', *Link: Eastern Suburbs*, September 1977.

133 H. Ramsay, 'Cycles of Control: Worker Participation in Sociological and Historical Perspective', *Sociology*, vol. 11, no. 3, September 1977, pp. 481–506; 'Invites for workers' control forum go to factory reps', *Tribune*, 16 July 1969, p. 12; 'Workers' Control: A Symposium', *Australian Left Review*, no. 2, April–May 1969, p. 11.

134 Central Industrial Secretariat, *Industry and Society*; Central Industrial Secretariat, *Communication, Consultation, Negotiation*, ca. 1973; Liberal Party of Australia, *Worker Participation or Workers' Control?* Sydney, Liberal Party of Australia, 1973, p. 2.

135 D.H. Giles, *Worker Participation in Australia: the Motives, Philosophy and Practice: A Study Commissioned by the Australian Institute of Management*, [Adelaide?] Australian Institute of Management, 1977, p. 13; N. Dufty, 'Industrial Democracy in Australia', *International Studies of Management and Organisation*, vol. 17, no. 2, 1987, p. 11.

136 'Chrysler: No Participation', *Tribune*, 19–25 March 1976, p. 12.

137 'First Ethnic Shop Committee', *Link: Western Suburbs Metal Workers Bulletin*, March 1977; 'Bans and Sitdown at IMCO: Lockout Fails', *The Link: Eastern Suburbs Metal Workers Bulletin*, November–December 1976.

138 D.H. Giles, *Worker Participation in Australia*, pp. 12, 14.

139 D. Hull, 'Job Redesign at ICI Australia', pp. 79, 81.

140 M. Barratt-Brown, 'The Institute for Workers' Control,' in Tony Simpson (ed.), *Resist Much, Obey Little: A Collection in Honour of Ken Coates* [np], Spokesman Books, 2012, p. 49; H. Braverman, *Labor and Monopoly Capital*, p. 39.

Chapter 9

141 V. Wallis, 'Workers' Control and Revolution', in I. Ness and D. Azzellini (eds), *Ours to Master*, Haymarket Books, 2011, p. 10.

142 S. Bull. 'Militants discuss building fighting unions', *Green Left Weekly*, 17 November 1993.

143 C. Oakley, 'The rise and fall of the ALP left in Victoria and NSW', *Marxist Left Review*, no 4, Winter 2012.

144 D. Kerin, interviewed by Sam Oldham, 'Dave Kerin on Worker Cooperatives and the Climate Emergency', *The Platform*, no. 3, 12 November 2014, http://www.anarchistaffinity.org/2014/11/dave-kerin-on-workers-cooperatives-and-the-climate-emergency/, accessed 10 October 2015.

BIBLIOGRAPHY

Articles

Bologna, S., 'Class Composition and the Theory of the Party in the German Workers' Councils', *telos: Critical Theory of the Contemporary*, no. 13 (Fall 1972), pp. 4–27.

Bowden, B., 'The Rise and Decline of Australian Unionism: A History of Industrial Labour from the 1820s to 2010', *Labour History: A Journal of Labour and Social History*, Issue 100 (May) 2011, pp. 51–82.

Bramble, T., 'Conflict, Coercion and Co-option: The Role of Full-Time Officials in the South Australian Branch of the Vehicle Builders Employees' Federation, 1967–80', *Labour History: A Journal of Labour and Social History*, Issue 63, 1992, pp. 135–154.

——, 'Trade Union Organization and Workplace Industrial Relations in the Vehicle Industry 1963 to 1991', *Journal of Industrial Relations*, vol. 35, no. 1 (March), 1993, pp. 39–61.

——, 'Australian Trade Union Strategies Since 1945', *Labour & Industry: A Journal of the Social and Economic Relations of Work*, vol. 11, Issue 03 (April), 2001, pp. 1–25.

Burgmann, V., 'The Green Bans Movement: Workers' Power and Ecological Radicalism in Australia in the 1970s', *Journal for the Study of Radicalism*, vol. 2, No. 1 (Spring), 2008, pp. 63–89.

Burgmann, V., R. Jureidini and M. Burgmann, 'Doing Without the Boss: Workers' Control Experiments in Australia in the 1970s', *Labour History: A Journal of Labour and Social History*, no. 103 (November), 2012, pp. 103–122.

Cottle, D. and A. Keyes, 'The Harco Stay-Put: Workers' Control in One Factory?' *The Hummer: Journal of the Australian Society for the Study of Labour History*, vol. 4, No. 1 (Summer), 2003–2004, http://asslh.org.au/hummer/vol-4-no-1/harco/ (accessed 3 June 2014).

Cronin, J.E., 'The "Rank and File" and the Social History of the Working Class', *The International Review of Social History*, vol. 34, Issue 01 (April), 1989, pp. 78–88.

Croucher, R. and M. Upchurch, 'Political congruence: A Conceptual Framework and Historical Case Study', *Labour History*, vol. 53, No. 2 (May), 2012, pp. 205–233.

Derber, M., 'Crosscurrents in Workers Participation', *Industrial Relations: A Journal of Economy and Society*, vol. 9, Issue 2, 1970, pp. 123–136.

———, 'Changing Union-Management Relations at the Plant Level in Australian Metalworking', *The Journal of Industrial Relations*, vol. 19, No. 1 (March), 1977, pp. 1–23.

———, 'Collective Bargaining: The American Approach to Industrial Democracy', *The Annals of the American Academy of Political and Social Science*, vol. 431 (May), 1977, pp. 83–94.

Dolack, P., 'Prague Spring: Workers' Control in a State-Owned Economy', *WorkingUSA*, vol. 16, Issue 3 (September), 2013, pp. 371–387.

Dufty, N., 'Industrial Democracy in Australia', *International Studies of Management and Organisation*, vol. 17, no. 2, 1987, pp. 10–16.

Freney, D., 'Workers' Control Perspectives', *Australian Left Review*, no. 39, 1973, pp. 3–6.

Frenkel, S.J., 'Explaining the Incidence of Worker Participation in Management: Evidence from the Australian Metal Industry', *Australian Journal of Management*, vol. 14, no. 2 (December), 1989, pp. 127–150.

Fry, E.C., 'Symposium: What is Labour History?' *Labour History: A Journal of Labour and Social History*, no. 12 (May), 1967, pp. 60–81.

Haskell, M., 'Green Bans: Worker Control and the Urban Environment', *Industrial Relations*, vol. 16, no. 2 (May), 1977, pp. 205–214.

Heino, B., 'The state, class and occupational health and safety: Locating the capitalist state's role in the regulation of OHS in NSW', *Labour & Industry*, vol. 23, no. 2, 2013, pp. 150–167.

Hutson, J., 'Workers Control', *Australian Left Review*, no. 1 (February–March), 1969, p. 8.

Hyman, R., 'The Sound of One Hand Clapping: A Comment on the "Rank and Filism" Debate', *The International Review of Social History*, vol. 34, Number 2 (August), 1989, pp. 309–326.

Lansbury, R.D., 'The Return to Arbitration in Australia: Recent trends in dispute settlement and wages policy in Australia', *International Labour Review*, vol. 117, no. 5, 1978, pp. 611–24.

Norman, D., 'Industrial Democracy in Australia', *International Studies of Management and Organisation*, 17, no. 2, 1987, pp. 10–16.

Norrell, R.J., 'After Thirty Years of "New" Labour History, There Is Still no Socialism in Reagan Country', *The Historical Journal*, vol. 33, No. 1 (March), 1990, pp. 227–238.

Oakley, C., 'The rise and fall of the ALP left in Victoria and NSW', *Marxist Left Review*, no. 4, Winter 2012, pp. 63–102.

Phelan, G., 'Shop Floor Organisation: Some Experiences from the Vehicle Industry', *Australian Left Review*, no. 78, 1981, pp. 10–20.

Political Research Group & Political Economy Movement, 'Workers, Trade Unions & Industrial Democracy', *Journal of Australian Political Economy*, vol. 3, 1978, pp. 82–88.

Price, R., '"What's In a Name?" Workplace History and "Rank and Filism"', *The International Review of Social History*, vol. 34, Issue 01 (April), 1989, pp. 62–77.

Quinlan, M. and R. Johnstone, 'The implications of de-collectivist industrial relations laws and associated developments for worker health and safety in Australia, 1996–2007', *Industrial Relations Journal*, vol. 40, no. 5 (September), 2009, pp. 426–443.

Ramsay, H., 'Cycles of Control: Worker Participation in Sociological and Historical Perspective', *Sociology*, vol. 11, no. 3 (September), 1977, pp. 481–506.

Ranis, P., 'Argentine Worker Cooperatives in Civil Society: A Challenge to Capital–Labor Relations,' *WorkingUSA*, vol. 13, Issue 1 (March), 2010, pp. 77–105.

Saunders, M., 'The Trade Unions in Australia and Opposition to Vietnam and Conscription: 1965-73', *Labour History*, no. 43, 1982, pp. 64–82.

Saunders, M. and N. Lloyd, 'Arbitration or collaboration? The Australasian Society of Engineers in South Australia, 1904-68', *Labour History: A Journal of Labour and Social History*, no. 101 (November), 2011, p. 123.

Sheldon, P. and L. Thornthwaite, 'The State, Labour and the Writing of Australian Labour History', *Labour History: A Journal of Labour and Social History*, no. 100 (May), 2011, pp. 83–104.

Westcott, M., 'Worker Control in the Australian Oil Industry', *Labour & Industry*, vol. 22, no. 4 (August–December), 2012, pp. 399–414.

Winn, P., 'Oral History and the Factory Study: New Approaches to Labor History', *Latin American Research Review*, vol. 14, no. 2, 1979, pp. 130–140.

Woodward, A.E., 'Industrial Relations in the 70s', *Journal of Industrial Relations*, 12, no. 2, 1970, pp. 115–129.

Zappala, G., 'The impact of the closed shop on the union movement: A preliminary view', *The Economic and Labour Relations Review*, vol. 2, no. 2, 1991, pp. 65–89.

Zeitlin, J., 'From Labour History to the History of Industrial Relations', *The Economic History Review*, New Series, vol. 40, no. 2 (May), 1987, pp. 159–184.

———, '"Rank and Filism" and Labour History: A Rejoinder to Price and Cronin', *The International Review of Social History*, vol. 34, Issue 01 (April), 1989, pp. 89–102.

———, '"Rank and Filism" in British Labour History: A Critique', *The International Review of Social History*, vol. 34, Issue 01 (April), 1989, pp. 42–61.

Books

Albinski, HS., *Politics and Foreign Policy in Australia: The Impact of Vietnam and Conscription*, Durham, N.C, Duke University Press, 1970.

Alperovitz, G., *America Beyond Capitalism: Reclaiming Our Wealth, Our Liberty and Our Democracy*, New Jersey, John Wiley & Sons, 2005.

Australian Manufacturing Workers' Union (ed.), *Talking Back: Reflections of Retired AMWU Activists*, Granville, NSW, AMWU, 2006.

Barratt-Brown, M., 'The Institute for Workers' Control', in Tony Simpson (ed.), *Resist Much, Obey Little: A Collection in Honour of Ken Coates*, (np), Spokesman Books, 2012.

Beasley, M., *Wharfies: The History of the Waterside Workers' Federation*, Halstead Press/Australian National Maritime Museum, 1996.

Berlanstein, L.R. (ed.), *Rethinking Labor History: Essays on Discourse and Class Analysis*, Chicago, University of Illinois Press, 1993.

Bramble, T., 'Managers of discontent', in Rick Kuhn (ed.), *Class and Struggle in Australia*, Pearson Education Australia, 2005.

Bramble, T., *Trade Unionism in Australia: A History from Flood to Ebb Tide*, Port Melbourne, Cambridge University Press, 2008.

Braverman, H., *Labor and Monopoly Capital: The Degradation of Work in the Twentieth Century*, New York & London, Monthly Review Press, 1974.

Brinton, M., *The Bolsheviks & Workers' Control 1917 to 1921*, London, Solidarity, 1970.

Burgmann, V., and M. Burgmann, *Green Bans, Red Union: Environmental Activism and the New South Wales Builders Labourers' Federation*, Sydney, University of New South Wales Press, 1998.

Carey, A., *Taking the Risk out of Democracy: Propaganda in the US and Australia*, Sydney, University of New South Wales Press, 1995.

Chomsky, N., *Government in the Future*, New York, Seven Stories Press, 2005.

Chomsky, N., *Chomsky on Anarchism*, 10th edn, Oakland and Edinburgh, AK Press, 2009.

Cleaver, H., *Reading Capital Politically*, Austin, University of Texas Press, 1979.

Coates, K., *Essays on Industrial Democracy*, Nottingham, Spokesman Books, 1971.

Coates, K., and T. Topham, *The New Unionism: The Case for Workers' Control*, London, Peter Owen, 1972.

Cohn-Bendit, D., trans. Arnold Pomerans, *Obsolete Communism: The Left-Wing Alternative*, London, Penguin Books, 1969.

Cole, K. (ed.), *Power, Conflict and Control in Australian Trade Unions*, Melbourne, Penguin Books, 1982.

Creighton, B., 'Law and Control of Industrial Conflict,' in K. Cole (ed.), *Power, conflict and control in Australian trade unions*, Ringwood, Pelican.

Crouch, C., *Class Conflict and the Industrial Relations Crisis: Compromise and Corporatism in the Policies of the British State*, Atlantic Highlands, NJ, Humanities Press, 1977.

Dawson, A., *Points and Politics. A History of the Electrical Trades Union of Queensland*, Brisbane, Colonial Press, 1977.

Dufty, N.F., *Industrial Relations in the Australian Metal Industries*, Sydney, West Publishing Corporation, 1972.

Eklund, E., *Steel Town: The Making and Breaking of Port Kembla*, Melbourne, Melbourne University Publishing, 2002.

Evans, R., *A History of Queensland*. New York, Cambridge University Press, 2007.

Foenander, O., *Shop Stewards and Shop Committees: A Study in Trade Unionism and Industrial Relations in Australia*, North Carlton, Melbourne University Press, 1965.

Ford, B. and D. Plowman, *Australian Unions: An Industrial Relations Perspective*, Melbourne, MacMillan, 1983.

Frenkel, S. J. (ed.), *Industrial Action: Patterns of Labour Conflict*, Sydney, George Allen & Unwin, 1980.

Frenkel, S.J. and A. Coolican, *Unions against Capitalism? A Sociological Comparison of the Australian Building and Metal Workers' Union*, Sydney, George Allen & Unwin, 1984.

Giles, D.H., *Worker Participation in Australia: the Motives, Philosophy and Practice: A Study Commissioned by the Australian Institute of Management*, [Adelaide?], Australian Institute of Management, 1977.

Goodrich, C.L. *The Frontier of Control: A Study in British Workshop Politics*, 2nd edn, London, Pluto Press, 1975.

Harman, C., *The Fire Last Time: 1968 and After*, 2nd edn, London, Bookmarks, 1998.

Healey, B., *Federal Arbitration in Australia: An Historical Outline*, Melbourne, Georgian House, 1972.

Huntley, P., *Inside Australia's Largest Trade Union*, Northbridge, Ian Huntley, 1978.

Hutson, J., *Penal Colony to Penal Powers*, Surry Hills, Amalgamated Engineering Union, 1966.

James, C.L.R., with R. Dunayevskaya and G. Lee, *State Capitalism and World Revolution*, 2nd edn., Chicago, Charles H. Kerr, 1986.

Jordan, D., *Conflict in the Unions: The Communist Party of Australia, Politics and the Trade Union Movement, 1945-1960*, Ultimo, NSW, Resistance Books, 2013.

Kurlansky, M., *1968: The Year that Rocked the World*, London, Vintage, 2005.

Lansbury, R.D., (ed.), *Democracy in the Work Place*, Melbourne, Longman Cheshire, 1980.

Mallory, G., *Uncharted Waters: Social Responsibility in Australian Trade Unions*, Annerley, QLD, Greg Mallory, 2005.

Markey, R., *In Case of Oppression: The Life and Times of the Labour Council of New South Wales*, Sydney, Pluto Press, 1994.

Marx, K., *Capital: A Critique of Political Economy, Vol. III*.

McGregor, c., *Profile of Australia*, London, Hodder & Stoughton, 1966.

McQueen, H., *Framework of Flesh: Builders' Labourers Battle for Health & Safety*, Adelaide, Ginninderra Press, 2009.

Moss, J., *Industrial Relations or Workers' Control: South Australian Experiences*, Adelaide, People's Bookshop, 1973.

Munro-Clark, M., *Communes in Rural Australia: The Movement Since 1970*, Sydney, Hale & Iremonger, 1986.

Murray, R. and W. Kate, *The Ironworkers: A History of the Federated Ironworkers' Association of Australia*, Sydney, Hale & Iremonger, 1982.

Ness, I. (ed.), *New Forms of Workers Organization: The Syndicalist and Autonomist Restoration of Class Struggle Unionism*, Oakland, PM Press, 2014.

Ness, I., *Southern Insurgency: The Coming of the Global Working Class*, London, Pluto Press, 2016.

Ness, I. and D. Azzelini (eds), *Ours to Master and to Own: Workers' Control from the Commune to the Present*, Chicago, Haymarket Books, 2011.

T. O'Lincoln, *Years of Rage: Social Conflicts in the Fraser Era*, Melbourne, Bookmarks, 1993.

———, *Into the Mainstream: The Decline of Australian Communism*, Carlton North, Red Rag Publications, 2009.

Owens, J. and J. Wallace, *Workers Call the Tune at Opera House*, Sydney Centre for Workers' Control, 1973.

Pearce, M., *Dockyard Militancy: A Study of the Conflict between the Navy and the Painters' and Dockers' Union*, Sydney, University of New South Wales, Department of Industrial Relations, September 1980.

Purdham, K., *A Century of Struggle: A History of the Electrical Trades Union of Australia Victorian Branch*, Flemington, VIC, Hyland House Publishing, 2002.

Rawson, D.W., *Unions and Unionists in Australia*, Sydney, George Allen & Unwin, 1978.

Roberts, E., *Workers' Control*, London, Allen & Unwin, 1973.

Rocker, R., *Anarcho-Syndicalism: Theory and Practice*, 6th edn, Oakland and Edinburgh, AK Press, 2004.

Reeves, A. and D. Andrew (eds), *Organise, Educate, Control: The AMWU in Australia, 1852-2012*, Clayton, Monash University Publishing, 2013.

Scalmer, S., *The Little History of Australian Unionism*, Carlton North, Vulgar Press, 2006.

Schmidt, M. and L. Van Der Walt, *Black Flame: The Revolutionary Class Politics of Anarchism and Syndicalism*, Oakland, CA, AK Press, 2009.

Seale, P. and M. McConville, *French Revolution 1968*, London, William Heinemann Ltd & Penguin Books, 1968.

Sheridan, T., *Mindful Militants: The Amalgamated Engineering Union in Australia 1920–1972*, Melbourne, Cambridge University Press, 1975.

Short, S., *Laurie Short: A Political Life*, Sydney, Allen & Unwin, 1992.

Simpson, T. (ed.), *Resist Much, Obey Little: A Collection in Honour of Ken Coates*, [np], Spokesman Books, 2012.

Turner, I., *In Union Is Strength: A History of Trade Union in Australia 1788–1978*, 2nd edn, Melbourne, Thomas Nelson, 1978.

Thomas, P., *Miners in the 1970s: A Narrative History of the Miners Federation*, Sydney, Miners Federation, 1983.

———, *Taming the Concrete Jungle: The Builders Labourers' Story*, Sydney, Australian Building Construction Employees & Builders Labourers' Federation, 1973.

———, *The Nymboida Story: The work-ins that saved a coal mine*, Sydney, Australian Coal & Shale Employees Federation, 1975.

Topham, T., *Productivity Bargaining and Workers' Control*, [Nottingham?] Institute for Workers' Control, 1968.

van der Velden, S., H. Dribbusch, D. Lyddon and K. Vandaele (eds), *Strikes Around the World, 1968–2005: Case Studies of 15 Countries*, Amsterdam, Aksant Academic Publishers, 2007.

Walker, K.F., *Australian Industrial Relations Systems*, Cambridge MA, Harvard University Press, 1970.

Wallis, V., 'Workers' Control and Revolution', in I. Ness and D. Azzelini (eds), *Ours to Master*, Haymarket Books, 2011, pp. 10–21.

Wright, C., *The Management of Labour: A History of Australian Employers*, Melbourne, Oxford University Press, 1995.

Wright, S., *Storming Heaven: Class Composition and Struggle in Italian Autonomist Marxism*, London, Pluto Press, 2002.

Zinn, H., *A People's History of the United States*, New York, Harper Perennial Modern Classics, 2010.

Melbourne Anarchist Archives: *development of Melbourne anarchism: drafts, documents & articles, 1966–1973*, [Melbourne?] ca. 1973.

Towards a Socialist Australia: How the labour movement can fight back: documents of the Socialist Workers Party, Sydney, Pathfinder Press, 1977.

Lectures, papers presented at meetings, and the like

Cameron, Clyde, 'Industrial Disputes in Australia: The Correct Perspective.' Address to the American Chamber of Commerce in Australia luncheon, Melbourne, November 30, 1973.

Cameron, Clyde, 'Managerial Control and Industrial Democracy: Myths and Realities.' Address to the AIM, NSW Division President's Dinner, Sydney, 20 August 1973).

Scott, Sir Walter, 'Looking into the 1970s.' Speech presented to the Autumn Seminar of the Royal Institute of Public Administration, Canberra, 1970.

Wang, K., Unit for Industrial Democracy, 'Current Debate', paper presented to the Health Service Personnel Officers' First National Seminar, Adelaide, 26 March 1976.

Manuscript Collections

AEU Melbourne District Committee, University of Melbourne Archives.

Records of the Gippsland Trades & Labour Council, Federation University Archives.

Records of the Ballarat North Railway Workshops Inter-Union Shop Committee, University of Melbourne Archives.

John Lysaght Collection, University of Wollongong Archives.

Stan Willis Collection, University of Melbourne Archives.

Records of the Combined Commonwealth Shop Stewards Committee Victoria, University of Melbourne Archives.

--- ALSO BY INTERVENTIONS ---

Stuff the Accord! Pay Up!
Workers' resistance to the ALP-ACTU Accord
Liz Ross
Interventions 2020

The Accord was a landmark program of restructuring Australian capitalism, a social contract between the union peak body, the Australian Council of Trade Unions and the social democratic Australian Labor Party. Earlier the metal workers union leader Laurie Carmichael proclaimed that the Accord was 'the pathway to socialism'. It was far from that. It pitched worker against worker, destroyed two unions, oversaw one of the greatest transfers of wealth from workers to employers, gutted union membership and the gains of previous decades.

While the Accord is generally portrayed as being welcomed by workers, in truth it was an agreement between the union leadership and the ALP, and many workers angrily resisted the many attacks on them. This story of resistance, from the left and workers' point of view, has not been told in full before. Ross' book, a left wing take on the Accord years, will link the many struggles and the real impact of the Accord on the Australian working class, as well as an analysis of the trade union leadership's role.

— ALSO BY INTERVENTIONS —

Radical Perth, Militant Fremantle
Edited by Charlie Fox, Alexis Vassiley,
Bobbie Oliver and Lenore Layman
Interventions 2020

This book tells 34 fascinating stories of radical moments In the cities' past, from as long ago as the 1890s and as recent as Occupy. The revised 2nd edition brings four new tales including the unknown story of striking Chinese seamen on the Fremantle waterfront, who faced brutal repression, but won support from Fremantle unionists. It also includes student radicalism at Curtin University (then WAIT), Perth's very-own Green Bans and solidarity with the famous strike of Aboriginal pastoral workers.

It also includes the 1998 Maritime Union of Australia dispute on Fremantle's waterfront, the revolutionary theatre of the Workers Art Guild; a riot of unemployed workers outside the Treasury building; rock concerts inside St Georges Cathedral; bodgies and widgies cutting up the dance floor at the Scarborough Beach Snake Pit; the Point Peron women's peace camp, and much more.

— ALSO BY INTERVENTIONS —

Years of Rage
Social Conflicts in the Fraser Era
Tom O'Lincoln
Interventions 2012

It's 1975, and Malcolm Fraser makes his ruthless grab for power. Workers resist, opening up seven years of bitter class conflict. From the upheavals of the Constitutional Crisis through the strikes in defence of Medibank and on to the 1981 "wage push", Tom O'Lincoln traces the industrial and political struggle, complemented with studies of social movements against oppression, unemployment, environmental destruction and war. Joh Bjelke-Petersen's crisis-ridden Queensland gets a chapter of its own, as do major debates on the left. The book shows how the exhaustion of the two sides after years of unrest set the scene for a Hawke Labor government that replace Fraser, yet brought nothing but disappointment to his opponents.

www.ingramcontent.com/pod-product-compliance
Lightning Source LLC
Chambersburg PA
CBHW070254010526
44107CB00056B/2457